The Least of These

By

Carrie and Neal Rozema

Contents

Under the apple tree I roused you;
there your mother conceived you,
there she who was in labor gave you birth.
Place me like a seal over your heart,
like a seal on your arm;
for love is as strong as death,
its jealousy unyielding as the grave.
It burns like blazing fire,
like a mighty flame.
Many waters cannot quench love;
rivers cannot wash it away.

Song of Songs 8:5-7

Prologue

There is a step in our home that has been a challenge. It is literally a step that leads out of the kitchen and down to a cold, hard tile by the back door. Cross the tile and you make it to our master bedroom, formally known by earlier tenants as the garage. Lovingly revamped with wood panel walls and plush brown carpeting, it makes for a cozy, cabin-like room at the end of the house for the whole family to bed down at night. So this step sees a lot of traffic. Tall and imposing, for a mother of little ones, it has had disaster written all over it. My oldest boy, Judge, learned how to negotiate the step as a toddler. Eventually, he mastered it and now leaps over it without a thought. My youngest, however, who just started toddling his way around the house a few months ago, has not yet conquered this giant.

Fortunately, this past summer, I found the perfect gate at a garage sale that sits tight and impenetrable at the top of the step. But inevitably, the gate will go down for one reason or another and my youngest will cross the kitchen and amble his way toward the precipice. I look over at him and say in my loudest and most intimidating voice, "NO, Joseph!", and he will stop and look back at me over his shoulder, a mischievous look in his eye that says, "I'm going over...you coming?" I walk over, scoop him up under his arms and place him safely on the other side of the ledge, watching him toddle his way into the bedroom. He has fallen once. One time when I didn't see him wander over to the step, when I didn't realize the gate was down and he was vulnerable. My brave little one year old decided to try it for himself, ending in a puddle of tears on the other side.

But today I was on the other side of the step, in our bedroom quietly putting freshly laundered clothes away in our closet, when I heard my little guy cry out. Distressed I was in another room, he came running through the kitchen and directly toward the ledge. I stopped what I was doing, held my arms out to my little Joseph and waited for him to meet me. He came careening across the floor, his eyes locked to mine as he cried out, "Ma Ma!" with his little arms stretched out in front of him. He didn't stop. He didn't wait to negotiate the step. He didn't wonder if I would catch him but instead made a running leap into my arms, his feet barely touching the floor before he took a mighty step off the ledge and into me. In that moment, I heard the voice of my Savior say to me, *This is how it is with those I call "the least of these."*

> *"Then the King will say to those on his right, 'Come, you who are blessed by my*

6

*Father; take your inheritance, the kingdom
prepared for you since the creation of the
world. For I was hungry and you gave me
something to eat, I was thirsty and you gave
me something to drink, I was a stranger and
you invited me in, I needed clothes and you
clothed me, I was sick and you looked after
me, I was in prison and you came to visit
me.' Then the righteous will answer him,
'Lord, when did we see you hungry and feed
you, or thirsty and give you something to
drink? When did we see you a stranger and
invite you in, or needing clothes and clothe
you? When did we see you sick or in prison
and go to visit you?' The King will reply,
'Truly I tell you, whatever you did for one of
the least of these brothers and sisters of
mine, you did for me.'"*

Matthew 25:34-40

"The least of these"...oh yes, Lord, that is how
it has been with me. I have toddled my way to the
top of very high ledges, negotiating the risk. I have
tumbled over, landing in a puddle of tears on the
other side. I have looked back at my Savior with a
mischievous look in my eye and how my Lord must
have known I was going over. How many times in
His mercy did He scoop me up and plant me safely
on the other side.

But in all those tumbles and in all the times He
reached down and picked me up, I have learned
beyond a shadow of a doubt, that going over that
step without Him will hurt. I have also learned that
when He is waiting for me on the other side, I can
run to him, eyes fixed and cry out, "Abba, Father!"

and He will catch me. I know this because I am one of "the least of these". I have been broken. I have been an outcast. I have been a sinner bent on doing things my way, only to find that without Him, I had lost my hope. I have been so damaged and so beaten that I now know, when left to my own devices, I will blow it every time. But I am not alone.

My husband and I are from the same camp. The place where losers go to play and those, whose failures are too enormous to cover up, find refuge in each other. It is the camp for the outcast, the criminal, the ugly, and the rejected. The place where every good Christian man and woman would be mortified to find themselves, and yet, it is a camp that Jesus frequently visits.

In this vile and desolate place, the King only sees potential. In this place, hearts are so broken that Jesus' healing touch is felt immediately. In this place, the will is so broken, that Jesus is *finally* able to have his complete and total way. It is here, among "the least of these", that Jesus reigns on high and the gates of hell cannot prevail against it.

1

Salvation Comes

Growing up in the South, everyone called themselves a Christian. Well, most did. Most got up early on Sunday morning to put on their favorite floral print dress, high heeled shoes and suit and tie to visit one of three main churches in our town- the Baptist, the Methodist or the Presbyterian.

We were Methodist and I would sit in church next to my mother and little brother, repeating the Doxology and singing the hymns, trying desperately to sit still for an hour and a half while the preacher spoke on and on about things I knew nothing about. Inevitably I would grab the hymnal in front of me, open up the front and back covers and attempt to find the exact middle by counting the pages on either side, one by one.

I believed in God. My grandmother made doubly sure of that. She had fallen in love with

Jesus in her sixties, shook off the ceremonial and religious to become a born again, sold out, all or nothing believer. She talked about Jesus constantly. Every conversation would inevitably lead back to Him and so I believed.

I remember my brother and I laying hands on a rusty old lawnmower that wouldn't start, praying in earnest that God would hear our prayer and turn the poor thing on....and watching it start right up. I remember lying in my bed and asking God for wisdom, having heard that it pleased God that Solomon had asked for that instead of fame and fortune, so I thought I would try to make Him happy too. I remember listing the Bible as one of the three things I would grab if my house was going down in flames. I knew Psalm 91, some basic David and Goliath stories and that was about it. Yet I clearly remember sitting on my mother's bed while she was out of town on a business trip, clasping hands with my little brother and grandmother and asking Jesus to come into my heart. It wasn't a momentous event but one that was burned in my memory at the age of ten.

My parents divorced when I was around the age of four. It was then Satan took advantage of all the tumult around me to whisper a lie into my young mind: *You are not worth sticking around for.* My father had left in torment. My mother had become a born again Christian and he had been raised a pastor's son. He saw all the hypocrisy and lovelessness he felt the church had to offer and wanted nothing to do with it. My mother was left in pain and some wounds would take years to heal. I believed in that moment that it was now up to me to make sure my mother and brother would survive it all. It was a heavy burden to bear but I picked it up willingly with my little arms and carried it faithfully.

As a tight family of three, we struggled to find our place in the world. With the help of my grandparents, we began to start over. My mom was smart and although starting at the bottom, her career flourished over time, steadily improving our situation. She had come to Jesus with fire and passion and had immediately felt the sting of rejection for it.

She looked to the church for support but was told early on that remarrying would be adulterous and so holding on to a dream of being happily remarried; she felt condemnation instead of mercy from her spiritual home. Our forays back to church were usually met with the feeling like we were on the outside looking in, watching the lives of those who seemed to have it all. All the while the enemy whispered in our ear that we were just not good enough to be there and we had little to prove otherwise. We would receive a sermon but church friends for our family were few, our brokenness too disconcerting for many.

So with salvation, the weak and shifting sands that were the foundation of my faith, and the lies in my head, I entered adolescence with a giant target on my back. I was a romantic and desperate for acceptance. I was a follower and insecure to my core. I longed to be stronger, braver, and to be loved. I was a recipe for disaster.

As the high school years began to set, I felt the taste of new freedoms. It was a strong desire not to be a burden to my already struggling single mother that kept me from so many of the evils quietly prowling around me. It was shyness and insecurity that kept some demons at bay, for a season, but the stage was being set. At the first real opportunity I was afforded, I was quick to drink and take my first hits of marijuana, hoping in this way to gain an edge and be part of something. The door was opened and I walked happily through.

I carried these new experiences with me to college in Arizona, my drive to prove I was worth something keeping my grades where they needed to be but opening myself up for disaster every weekend. I was experimental and excited...acid, ecstasy, mushrooms and fun. Avoiding drugs I thought might leash me into addiction, I played and partied and then lost my innocence to a boy with demons of his own.

There is nothing like a broken heart to drive home worthlessness in a person already struggling to believe they are worth anything. I gave myself away and learned that a lot more is taken then just a body; that flesh and bone is only a part, but the place that bleeds is within and the damage that gets done, flows blood, red and deep. No true romance and no happy ending, only the pain of rejection and slavery to someone who could not fix it. So as things began to unravel, I holed up in my room and darkness set in. I cried to my mom on the phone and, she, recognizing the pain of heartbreak, reminded me to read the Bible. I began to think again about Him and because I needed help climbing out of the hole I had fallen in, I picked up my Bible.

The university I attended sat up 7,000 ft high above sea level and behind sat a big, snow capped mountain that became my place of refuge. As many days as I could, I would grab my Bible, drive the 20 minutes up the mountain in search of a secluded spot. I would open up the Word and begin to read and although so much of what I read was beyond my ability to comprehend, I knew one thing. For that brief moment, sitting alone, outside with Bible in hand, I felt better. Lighter. Like maybe everything was going to be okay.

As I would drive back down the mountain, I would feel the peace recede as I re-entered my world of shame but that peace is what beckoned me back over and over again in the course of a year, at the end of which I could say, "I believe". I can't explain to you how I knew what I was reading was the Truth. There was no pastor, or friend to explain things to me in a way I could understand. I had no other books to look to or television programs to guide me. It was just me and Jesus, up on a mountain top and I was beginning to feel better.

But unfortunately, whenever the enemy sees progress being made, he ramps his efforts and draws a bigger target. I managed, through tears, to escape the torment of binding myself to someone who would not love me back. I could call myself Christian. I spent time with the Lord but the wounds of the enemy were still there: *You are not worth loving.*

I looked for love again, this time intent on making a "smart" decision. I found a new face that promised to love me and fell for it completely. No matter that I had to party harder to spend time with him or that most of the time we were together, he was high on something. He was a pastor's son. He believed in God but he was like me. He didn't buy into the whole church thing, which was really just code for we can still do whatever we want, where we want, when we want. I followed him to Oregon as we tried to pursue dreams. We married in a ceremony with six people; me, in corduroys with a bouquet of wildflowers and my mom crying on the other end of the phone. It was the beginning of an unholy mess. Yet there was something about marriage that made me want to try a little harder with the Lord. Something that made me want to have my feet a little more firmly planted than they had been. I started going to church. He went off the deep end.

It was only a few months after the wedding that everything started to deteriorate. As I began attending church for myself for the first time, he plunged headfirst into a deep depression, refusing to get off the couch sometimes for days and gone so many nights. I would lay in bed awake, tormented and sick to my stomach, wondering where he was, who he was with and what was he doing. When he would make it home, I threw things, screamed and pointed fingers all to no avail. He ran farther and farther away from me, coming back sporadically in remorse, confessing the sins of the past few weeks, only to leave days later into the great unknown.

In the midst of it all, I continued to learn new and wonderful things about Christ at a small church in Portland. There were many things that I had not fully understood having just read the Bible on my own. But, as years went by, I struggled to attend, trying to put on a happy face and confiding in only a few. I recognized quickly that my life was a far cry from those around me. I drank more, smoked more and cried constantly.

Finding myself in the pit once again, I poured myself into the Bible, spending hours reading and journaling to try to make sense of some of the chaos I was living in. Would God want me to leave my marriage? Would He be disappointed in me if I just couldn't stay anymore? Would He ever be pleased with me again if this all ended in divorce? I thought I knew the answer so I stayed and stayed and stayed. Then, I broke.

The first time I left, I remember packing all my things into my blue Chevy S10 and driving three days back to my mom's house in Chicago, where she had moved several years before. It wasn't a real attempt to leave. I always thought I would go back but this at least would teach him a lesson. He would see that he would lose me if he didn't try to get better and he would change.

And he *was* upset; the house began to cave in around him when all the effort I had put into holding things together melted away. We signed an unofficial marriage contract with our parent's help, promised to fulfill our end of the bargain and made attempts to repair the marriage. I went back and on the day I arrived, after driving three days, I came home to an empty house and a husband passed out at a friend's home across town. I dropped my face in my hands, leaned my back against the wall and slid to the floor. I was trapped again.

It was three months later, the Lord delivered me. Everything had become increasingly dangerous. He would call me, high, threatening to kill himself out in the woods somewhere. He was seeing things, people in the yard in the middle of the night waving to him. He had guns, a couple of them, and he really didn't want me to leave. I was scared. Finally, one morning my dad called me on the phone, patiently instructing me that my situation was not going to change and the Lord spoke to my heart, *It's time to go.* I prayed, "Lord, how can I leave. He'll never let me leave." It was not a few hours later that one of his friends called him at work, inviting him to a party on the coast, hours away. He would have to leave that day if he wanted to go and he desperately wanted to go. Within a matter of minutes he had made plans to be gone for the weekend and the next day, I packed up my stuff in the blue Chevy S10 for the last time, kissed the dogs goodbye and left for good.

I still remember waking up in a hotel room, somewhere between Portland and Chicago, with guilt and fear laying into me. Would he kill himself? Would it be my fault? The Lord spoke tenderly to me, *Keep going.* So I did, nearly collapsing on the floor of my mother's home from the weight of exhaustion. I was home, I was safe and God had rescued me.

2

Mary Magdalene

Jesus traveled about from one town and village to another, proclaiming the good news of the kingdom of God. The Twelve were with him, and also some women who had been cured of evil spirits and diseases: Mary (called Magdalene) from whom seven demons had come out...

Luke 8:1-2

Mary stood on the side of a hill watching from a distance. She had followed Jesus from Galilee, witnessing over and over again what the prophets foretold so many years before. The wind whipped around her hair, slapping her face as she looked on. Her Savior, hanging from a cross, just took His last breath. His head dropped and the sky became dark. Mary doubled over in pain. Under her feet the earth began to tremble. Rocks split and tombs broke open. Bodies, raised from death to life, broke forth from their earthly graves and in the Temple, the curtain split from top to bottom.

"Surely He was the Son of God!" said the soldier at the foot of the now crucified Christ. Yes, He was the Son of God but she did not need to see all these signs and wonders to know that. She had known this for a while and for that reason, had abandoned everything to follow Him.

It was many months before that Mary had collided with the kingdom of God. Her demons were in a panic. Jesus had been walking from town to town, village to village with throngs of people following in His wake. People were getting healed left and right and all of hell was in an uproar. Screeching and begging for mercy, demons were being rebuked and sent packing with a simple command from the King. And the tormented, no longer at their mercy, were becoming free.

Mary Magdalene had seven demons residing in her small frame, and she carried all the marks and scars to show for it. A victim to their lies, she had held court with them for so long that she had lost the ability to hold up her head or dream of something better. She was desperate and alone in her misery, but not unseen.

Before Jesus at His feet, the demons had knocked her down before taking flight, wailing and gnashing their teeth as they went. She looked up and took the outstretched hand of her Savior, as He helped her to stand. Freedom and tears, she would follow Him anywhere. Mary had been given hope for the first time in what seemed like forever and she knew exactly who was the author of it.

Faithful Mary of Magdalene then followed Jesus from town to town, one of several women who found healing at His word. They worked tirelessly to support Jesus and His men from their own means and followed Him from Galilee all the way to Jerusalem to care for Him. And here He was now, naked, bleeding and hanging from a cross. The only person in this world who dared to look lovingly in her eyes and tell her she was worth something, when even she couldn't believe it to be true. The man she had walked so many miles with and had so carefully tended to was now being ravaged by wolves.

When the end had come, reality stuck her like a hard fist in the stomach. Up until then she had waited for a miracle, hoping and praying for someone or something to get Him down off that cross, to end His suffering and bring Him home. But that had not happened and the weight of losing Him fell like a mighty blow.

Her grief drove her to wake early after the Sabbath, at the first break of dawn to bring spices and tend to her Savior's lifeless body. She would be close to Him again, even if in a tomb. Only now, to her unraveling, He was not where He was supposed to be. Again, an earthquake trembled, but this time, angels appeared. In her complete and total devotion to Jesus, Mary became highly favored, being chosen to receive the revelation about the risen King from the mouth of angels. Then Jesus, hidden from her eyes until just that moment, spoke her name, and in an instant, she knew it was true. Her Savior was alive and as she ran to cling to Him as her heart had done so many times before, she was stopped by a Jesus no longer of this world. Stopped, but sent on a mission: *Go and tell the others what you have seen.* Mary delivered of seven demons, now His messenger elect and first to behold the one true King.

3

The Courtship

When the world around you crumbles, you have two choices. You can hide your face in your knees and surrender or stand up and try to climb your way out. I was climbing but the road was treacherous. Bankruptcy and divorce loomed large but Jesus held tight my hand, steering me left and right until one day, my footing became a little surer. Every night I would pour myself into His Word, journaling for hours and letting His love wash over me. I longed for Sunday mornings at my mother's church when I could raise my hands and thank Him for second chances. He was everywhere with me and I wanted to go nowhere without Him.

The end came swiftly to my marriage. No contest and no reason to fight, he had moved in with another and it was broken. The King spoke softy, *I have divided you to serve a greater purpose,* and so my heart had peace. Fresh waves of sorrow would wash over me from time to time, watching couples on the street, or families at the mall, only to be quieted by gentle assurances from the Lord. Wounds began to heal and I began to stand more upright. Brokenness led to sweet surrender and I clung to Jesus with all of my heart. I trusted Him and He took care of me, having rescued me like a white knight, He now wiped all my tears with His Word.

As He nursed me back to health, we made a deal. I was never, ever going to go anywhere without Him again and if He intended for me to spend my life with someone, He and only He could make that choice for me. I was prepared to walk this world with only Him at my tender age of 25. I was clearly too broken to choose a mate on my own, so incapable of right choices in this department that I couldn't fake it or pretend. The fruit of my decisions were out there for the entire world to see. It was humbling and embarrassing. I wanted my life to be in His hands now, the only safe place to be.

The day I met Neal, I was waiting for my next table, back against the wall with my hair pulled tight in a pony tail, my server apron neatly pressed against black slacks. I nudged his brother, my co-worker, gently teasing him about his family coming for a visit, only to be led by the hand in one swoop over to Neal's table for introductions. It was over in an instant but Neal came back.

I would see him visit from time to time, watching me out of the corner of his eye. I was flattered but not moved. Neal had all the girls in the restaurant in an uproar, melting and fawning over him even as he would look past. Good looking and master of his environment, Neal was the lead bartender at the local establishment, his indifference to their attention just making him more desirable to the girls by the moment. Needless to say, I felt *certain* this man would not be God's choice for me. So God only knows why, one day, when Neal came into the restaurant for a visit, I smiled back.

When someone has lived so long in the world, doing things a certain way, even a heart tendered to Jesus has trouble shaking loose of old patterns. I was going to church, but I wasn't a pretty picture. I was young and in love with Jesus, but in many righteous eyes, broken and a fool. The world I knew before was competing with the kingdom of God, offering acceptance and friendship when, often times, I would walk into the church feeling the weight of my singleness, the pain of rejection and the dirt of my past. I struggled to find a place. I was labeled a single but in my heart knew that I didn't feel led to present myself to the world as such, with all that it implied.

I wanted to help people, serve God in the places where my testimony might save someone else from similar mistakes. I looked to work with youth groups but, as the news of my divorce came to light in the interview for volunteers, I saw a shadow pass over their face and knew that I would not be receiving a follow up phone call. Somehow fitting in on the outside was easier than finding a place to call home in the church my Jesus loved. I felt broken, tarnished and hard to place. However, the Lord held tight to me, leading me to a small group of men and women with a heart for prison ministry. I played the guitar and worshipped with those who were crushed in spirit and felt a measure of camaraderie.

But I had also been in enough bars to know exactly how to blend. I knew the etiquette and lay of the land. So when Neal asked me to come and meet him for a drink, I went and felt...special. I sat cautiously at the edge of the bar as I waited for him to get off work. I pulled out a cigarette and it was lit before I could even fumble for my lighter. I knew I was flirting with trouble but I was determined to not open the door so wide I couldn't shut it again. And he, watching my every move, was taking copious notes with his eyes, a new drink in front of me before the other was half gone.

I prayed Jesus would be with me in this place. I felt danger and I needed Him. His great love protected me so that when Neal walked me to my car, he never made a move, but instead. graciously asked me to dinner. I accepted, went home and prayed, *God, protect me.* I felt weak and uncertain, treading very dangerous ground. On my knees, I invited the Lord into my newfound situation, pleading and begging Him to remove Neal from my life if I was in trouble, to give me good direction, to light my path.

So on the night of our first date, I remembered God, did as I was led, and let Neal have it. Faithfully unleashing my weapon, I began my speech, "I need you to know that I am a Christian...I go to church and it's very important to me...I'm not going to be any fun..." Boom, boom, boom and then, I waited. He had been listening quietly, leaning back on his chair and when I was done, he leaned forward and said, "Perfect, that is just what I am looking for..." Boom. Not quite sure

I had heard him right, I eyed him suspiciously. He quoted John 3:16 to me and we were off, a bottle of wine between us to numb the sheer panic of possibility.

I asked God to lead, protect, and guide me. I promised Him that I would not make this decision without Him. I would trust His judgment and lean on His protection. I would not date someone based on outward appearances and I would not walk through that door without some kind of confirmation. And here was Neal, the farthest thing from a "safe" choice, sitting across from me, passing the first test. I was excited and scared to death.

From that evening on we started to spend a lot of time together. Clutching my heart with both my hands, I looked to heaven constantly. "Father, You decide," I said, "Father, I put him on Your altar." We started to fall in love. Then we went too far, the enemy's lies from my youth still looming large in my head...*You are not worth sticking around for.* I went a path I had taken before and begged Him for forgiveness. Deeply convicted, I backed off. We looked for churches together, slipped into sin again, and I begged the Lord for help.

It was a mess; climbing and slipping all the way, I tried desperately to right wrongs and position us well for a life together. Night after night I would beg God not to leave me, not to give up on me. The Lord slogged through the mud with me, never giving up. He spoke to me in a whirlwind, beckoned me forward, called me higher and took my hands when I was knocked down and covered in dirt. Leading me, faithfully, every day until at last He whispered to my heart, *Hold on to Me...this is your husband.* Neal asked me to marry him and I accepted, wholeheartedly, clearly knowing what the Lord had told me.

Then, bad things started to happen. First, Neal lost his job. I wasn't crazy about the whole bartending thing anyway; but then I started to notice chunks of the day and night where Neal seemed to disappear. A half hour errand would take three. He always had a reason; a great story to back it up, but it became increasingly more common. Then there were times when I looked up in his eyes and recognized a familiar sight, red rings encircling a vacant stare, like Neal was somewhere else.

He was sick a lot, sometimes shaking so bad that we would just try to wrap up on the couch to keep warm. I would wake sometimes to find Neal sleeping on the floor, moving there to avoid waking me with all his thrashing about. There were signs and suspicions, but nothing concrete. Then, money started to disappear. He had a great reason the first time I realized he withdrew money from my account. "Rent was due...my mom really needed the money...I didn't want to wake you." Then it happened again and I was mad. He apologized and swore he would never do it again. When money went missing from me a third time, I called it off.

I knew now that something was really wrong. I knew I could not be in a relationship with someone who could steal from me. My heart was broken again. I had let my guard down believing Neal was the one but clearly that wasn't the case. But more than that and even more debilitating was the obvious fact that I was too broken, too much of a sinner to clearly hear from God. My sins were too many and I was just fooling myself to believe that

God could still lead me in the midst of all my shame. I poured my heart out to God, sobbing in repentance for how I had so obviously disappointed Him, the pain of it feeling more than I could bear. Then, in the quiet of my room, I heard the Lord say to me, *I want you to forgive him for everything.* He not only said it, He put it so deep inside me that in an instant, peace filled my heart. The crying abated and I sat stunned in silence. Forgive him? Yes, that was what He said, and all of the sudden I was desperate to find Neal, desperate to forgive him for all that had happened.

I grabbed my coat, jumped in the car and drove to his small, dark apartment. Finding he wasn't there, I went looking for him, walking out the back door toward the retention pond behind his house where we had spent hours holding hands and falling in love. At the crest of the hill rising above the water, I saw a dark profile sitting against the night sky. It was cold and a gentle mist was falling on both of us as I climbed the embankment and took a seat next to him. He looked sideways to see me, head hanging low, but did not move. I leaned into him, "Neal, I don't know how this is going to work but God just told me to forgive you for everything…so that is what I am going to do." Quiet for several minutes, he looked up at me and I wrapped my arms around him. We descended the hill, back to our lives, and I waited, wondering how God was going to protect me in all this forgiveness.

Two weeks later, Neal was arrested.

4

Demoniac of the Tombs

When Jesus got out of the boat, a man with an evil spirit came from the tombs to meet him. This man lived in the tombs, and no one could bind him any more, not even with a chain.

Mark 5:2-3

The demons were shrieking, their voices so loud and shrill, he felt as if his vocal chords would snap. He tumbled to the ground before the one they called Jesus and the spirits, writhing inside, were in a panic. "Why are you bothering me, Jesus, Son of the Most High God?" they screamed. They held him down and, powerless, he played instrument to their hideous voice, a role he had played so many times before. "Come out!" Jesus commanded and the demons convulsed, contorting his body as he twisted in pain. This Jesus had them on their knees, something that had never happened before.

He couldn't remember how long it had been since he left the warmth of his home to take up residence here among the tombs, an asylum of horrors for anyone who dared to pass through. He didn't know how long it had been but he saw the marks of many years. There were deep, penetrating scars around his wrists and ankles, the result of chains and shackles meant to contain the beasts that lived inside him. All to no avail, for in their rage, they were as strong as a thousand men and could snap the metal like twigs.

He begged for rest, prayed into the darkness that they would be contained if only for him to take some comfort in shelter, to cover the shame of his nakedness for a moment, even if it meant chains. But the prayers would go unanswered and he inevitably would be sent hurdling into the dark wilderness with rocks and thorns tearing at his feet as he ran, the terrible pain a symptom of his madness.

Bloody and broken, he would pass out among the tombs, his body eventually forcing him into sleep, where he would again be tormented in his dreams with visions of horror and death. His eyes would snap open at the sound of approaching footsteps or the low hum of voices. He would come hurdling out of the darkness again, screaming and pounding his fists. In one leap, he could attack his unsuspecting victim, beating them with rocks, sticks, or whatever was close at hand, his impulse to kill overpowering any rational thought or memory of love. No one was strong enough to subdue him and so he wandered this way, day and night, his screams pealing through the sacred space while his own hands beat himself bloody.

He was crouched at a distance when he saw Jesus climb out of His boat and walk ashore. A voice resonated deep inside him that had shaken him to the core. This voice said, "Run, now!" In an instant, he took off running, a mad dash to this figure who had just made His first few footsteps on dry land. He didn't know why he was running so fast and furious down toward the water, only that he seemed propelled there by a force different from the ones he had grown so accustomed to. It was a force that seemed to come from a different place, a place that felt a little like... hope. On his hands and knees now before Jesus, he could see that his enemies were somehow losing control.

"You have no right to torture us before God's appointed time!" the demons screamed into the air. Legion was their name because there were so many. They begged Jesus to be sent into the herd of pigs gathered restlessly on the side of the shore. Jesus conceded, and at the sound of the word, "Go!", the demons left in a torrent of black air and death, their former host collapsing as his body, having been lifted and suspended for a moment, came crashing back to the earth with great force. Lying motionless on the ground, he heard the thunder of the running hoofs, the splash and thrashing of water, as the pigs took off running down the steep embankment, drowning themselves in despair. There was confusion, chaos, and then silence.

The man lay there, afraid to move. His breath was loud in his ears, the smell of earth in his nostrils. Slowly, in the quiet, he began to lift his head, just a little, if only to get his bearings and run again if he needed to. His eyes looked up and saw the dusty, sandaled feet of the one they called the Son of God. They continued upward as he placed his palms on the sandy earth and slowly lifted his head, his body responding with surprising lightness. A hand came out to meet him, gently helping to lift his tattered frame. Higher he rose until he was able to lock on the most beautiful eyes he had ever seen. "Get this man some clothes," Jesus said, and the man was whisked away in a sea of strangers, clothing him, dressing his wounds, and cleaning the dirt from his face and hands. His thoughts were coming clearly now, the voices that had tormented and dominated his mind suddenly quiet. And the peace…he felt warmth from the inside out, his heart radiating stillness he had never known before. He sat this way at the feet of Jesus and prayed he would be able to stay there forever.

The crowds started to gather. He felt the weight of their stares and heard the anxious whisperings. Alarm swept through the townspeople as they watched him sit calmly with his Savior. The magnitude of what just happened moved over them like a wave and panic was setting in. A man with this enormous power would not soon be forgotten but for now, He needed to leave. What more might this Son of God do? What more sacrifices would have to be made? What more possessions lost? They begged Him to go. But as Jesus turned to make His way back to the boat, back across the sea, the man leapt to his feet. Jesus was going nowhere without him.

Jesus turned and smiled with full assurance. In an instant, this man knew he no longer had anything to fear. His new love for Jesus would now protect him in the dark places; his freedom was guaranteed by his newfound faith. "Let me come with you," he begged, and Jesus, tenderly placing His hand on his shoulder said, "Friend, I have a more important task for you. Go back to your family and friends and tell them the wonderful things God has done for you. Tell them how merciful God has been and don't be afraid. God is with you." He finished and smiled knowingly at him, His eyes twinkling with love and tenderness.

At this, the man began to smile. He took a few steps back and as Jesus boarded the boat, turned on his heel and began to run. But this time, he was running home, back to the people he had once known and back into town. This new messenger of God would tell everyone he knew about this man called Jesus. He would never stop talking about what God had done for him. He would go through the entire city until everyone heard his testimony, could see this living proof of a Savior, and believe.

5

The Call

The elevator rose three floors, the door opened and our unhappy group slowly filed out. Before us were ten small cubicles, each one furnished with a metal stool, a phone hanging on the left side wall and a glass partition to the front. We slowly split apart, each small family picking a seat in which to see their loved one.

Hesitantly I sat down, angry and scared. I had never been to a place like this before, never even knew where the Dupage County Jail was located. There were so many hoops to jump through to even get this far. There were select days and hours we were allowed to visit inmates, certain documentation required and a long wait with many other heartbroken and shell shocked families, each trying to navigate a terrifying system. I waited for hours watching a mother cry softly in her seat;

someone's brother sitting with elbows on his knees, looked up only occasionally as an officer would read off the list of names that would be next in line to board the elevator for a visit. We traveled up together, strangers sharing a very real pain.

Sitting on our stools, we waited for our inmates to flood in. At the sound of a door opening, the other side of the partition came alive with men in orange jumpsuits scrambling to find their family or friend and take a seat. We only had thirty minutes to talk until the following week when we would be allowed to visit again, so not one moment could be wasted. Neal sat down quickly across from me, sadness and fear mixed with the excitement of my visit all played across his face. Neal had been in jail exactly five days and I put on my best mad face.

Five days before, my life had been rocked to the core. I received a phone call from Neal, very brief and from a pay phone, saying he was at a police station. There was a big misunderstanding but they were holding him for questioning. I couldn't believe my ears. He was with a friend working out at a local gym and had gotten picked up for stealing a wallet out of a gym locker. He assured me he would be home soon, that there was no reason to worry, and so I went to his apartment after I got off of work and waited for him to come home. I waited and waited but no sign of Neal. His mother was the one to inform me that he had been transferred to the Dupage County Jail; they were working on finding a way to bond him out and Neal was facing some real trouble.

I was in shock. Bond him out? I barely knew what that meant but it all sounded a lot more serious than I had originally been led to believe. I went home that night trying to make sense of all the new information until later that evening I received a call. A former friend of the family, a girl I had spent some time with throughout the eight months Neal and I had dated, felt like I was a nice girl and someone who had a right to know.

Previously, Neal had sat down with me after about four months of dating to let me know that he had been to jail before. He wanted me to hear it from him and told me a story about being in the wrong place at the wrong time, a series of unfortunate circumstances that landed him in the Illinois Department of Corrections for several years. I cried big tears as he told me his story, just imagining him behind bars, charged with something that was not his doing and living life as a prisoner. But that, I learned, was only a part of the story and she began to unload on me, with great fear and trembling, all the things she knew to be true of Neal.

This was not Neal's first time being locked up, nor was it his second. In fact, Neal had a long and established history of being in and out of jail for crimes related to theft. Not only that, but Neal had been stealing for a reason, as he also had a long and established history of using heroin. Heroin. Her voice continued on the other end of the line but I was still hanging on that word. I interrupted her, "Neal has a heroin problem?" I couldn't believe it. Was she sure? Then pieces started to come together in my mind and everything started to make sense. *Oh no*, I thought to myself, *not heroin*.

I was in high school one afternoon, many years before, watching a program about the devastating effects of heroin. The program told the story of a young man and his mother; the young man experimenting with heroin in high school only to quickly become a full fledged addict while his mother worked tirelessly and for years to get him into the right programs for help. She had even sent him to some strange island for rehabilitation, away from everything, only for him to come back home and fall right back into addiction again. I remembered the words being burned across the screen at the end of the program, "Only 2 to 3% of people with a heroin addiction ever achieve sobriety..." So when I heard her say Neal had a heroin addiction, to me, it was a death sentence.

I had done drugs before but never heroin. I went to Al Anon meetings while living with my ex-husband, learned about addiction, co-dependency and the Twelve Step Program but no one had ever discussed the word heroin. To me it was a place with no hope, so when I heard heroin, my world stopped. As I hung up the phone, rage and pain flooded my heart. So overwhelmed by grief and disappointment, it was all I could do to answer the phone when Neal finally called me again from County Jail. I laid into him and told him everything I knew; that he was a liar and I was heartbroken. I told him I never wanted to see him again, hung up the phone and sobbed for days.

Three days later, I sat across the kitchen table from a dear friend and mentor of mine from church. I was crying to her, beside myself. How could this all be? I had known something wasn't right but I trusted God. I asked Him to guide and protect me. I had made so many mistakes, but He had held up my head and quietly assured me of His presence. But that, I reasoned again, could not be because God would never lead me to marry a thief and a heroin addict.

I questioned myself and my ability to hear the voice of God all over again. I sat crying, burying my face in my hands. Then my friend, trying herself to understand, said tenderly to me, "Well maybe God wants you to pray and intercede for this man." The instant it came out of her mouth, the Lord exploded a bomb in my heart. I lifted my head. Yes, that was *exactly* what the Lord wanted me to do. I asked my friend what exactly that meant and she proceeded to look through a small library in her home to fish out all the books she had on spiritual warfare and intercessory prayer.

My heart started burning within me, growing lighter with each passing moment. The Holy Spirit began convicting and moving me, inspiring me to action. In that moment, I knew I was to pray and intercede for Neal. Heroin was not hopeless as long as God was with me and so armed with prayers, I left her house and headed home to try and figure out what on earth this all meant.

Coming home, I turned on the small lamp above my bed and started to read. What did it mean to intercede? How does one pray for someone with addiction? I faithfully copied down several prayers, repeating them over and over again in the quiet of my room. They were prayers that began with, "I speak to you Satan, to the powers, and principalities, to spiritual wickedness in high places and to the demonic forces assigned to Neal. I take authority over you in the mighty name of Jesus..." They were prayers that demanded Neal was set free, that called on ministering spirits of God to go forth in the name of Jesus and help Neal in whatever way needed. They were prayers for Neal's complete and total deliverance from the enemy and for salvation. As I prayed in this way, my heart began to grow and burn for my captive, for the one I loved who was being held hostage by Satan. I was filled to overflowing with new hope.

So when the day came for me to be able to visit Neal at the Dupage County Jail, I was ready to say, "God wants me to stand with you and pray. If you are willing to do the right thing, then I will do it with you." Neal, having sat down on the other side of the glass partition not knowing what to expect, heard these words come out of my mouth and his expression lightened. Yes, he was willing to do anything. He was so tired of his life, so ready for something different and something better. He was ready to do anything because, little did I know, Jesus had already been doing a lot behind the scenes, in the quiet of Neal's cell.

6

An Adulterous Woman

Jesus went to the Mount of Olives. At dawn he appeared again in the temple courts, where all the people gathered around him, and he sat down to teach them. The teachers of the law and the Pharisees brought in a woman caught in adultery. They made her stand before the group...

John 8:1-3

She sat there with her shame all night long, fear and loathing her only friends. Now everyone would know; her worst nightmares were coming true. They took her forcibly the night before, dragging her kicking and screaming into the night air with nothing but a sheet to cover her nakedness. Her lover watched in horror as she was removed from his bed, but made not one move to stop it. Caught in the act, his mind quickly shifted to thoughts of his wife and family, his reputation, his life. But for whatever reason, maybe his prominence in the community, maybe because his wife came from a wealthy family, they seemed more interested in her than him.

He had noticed her from across the room, a young girl with dark, brown eyes cast down, sweetly serving the guests at the party. He watched the way her hair tumbled over her shoulders in waves, the way her dress rose and fell on her small frame as she moved quietly around the room. Beautiful. He wanted her desperately from that moment on and every thought since had been to have her, some way, somehow.

The two of them had tried to be so careful. He knew his family would be gone for several days visiting relatives in the neighboring town. It seemed the perfect opportunity to finally be able to fulfill every secret desire they had. And it had seemed perfect. He whispered soft words of love to her in the late hours of the night, promising her that one day they would leave all these attachments behind and be together forever. She believed him and let herself be taken away in passion. No one had ever spoken such words of love to her, not even her own father. She had spent most of her life at the mercy of others, seeming sent to misuse and abuse her. She craved affection in any form and had finally found it with him.

Yes, he was married. But he told her his wife was a hard woman. Always complaining and never affectionate, he tried to be the perfect husband but his wife was never happy. They were not intimate and no longer even spoke as friends, and he professed to have finally found both in her.

Adulterous. An ugly word and it hung like a black cloud over her head. They brought her to a small chamber where she remained all night. His wife must have found out, must have made arrangements to "take care" of her, a powerful woman in the community with powerful friends. And she…was nothing.

The Jewish leaders came early the following morning. Throwing a tattered robe at her, they commanded she get dressed. The penalty for adultery was stoning. She knew this and her fingers trembled as she attempted to dress and smooth her hair. There would be a trial; she would be found guilty, and then condemned. They grabbed her roughly by the arms, pushing and dragging her all the way to the Temple. Then, to her horror, they threw her in front of the crowd.

Many people had gathered that day and she could feel the penetrating stare of every last one of them. But the Pharisees and teachers of religious law seemed concerned with only one in the crowd of people gathered there, a teacher named Jesus. They shouted at Him a question, "Teacher, this woman was caught in the act of adultery. In the Law Moses commanded us to stone such women. Now what do you say?" The silence in the room was deafening as all waited in anticipation to hear the fate of the scorned and defiled woman. Everyone waited and, when no response was given, the religious leaders shouted louder.

Her eyes that had been scanning the room feverishly as she struggled to keep covered under the makeshift dress, finally fixed on the man that seemed at the center of the interrogation. All attention had shifted from her to this man, Jesus, stooped down and writing in the dust with His finger. This teacher clearly knew the Law; it was unlawful to write on the Sabbath but words in the dust were permissible. Surely He would know that the Law said she must die. She could not see what He was writing, only seeing the frame of a man, hunched over in the dirt, holding her fate in the palm of His hands. Finally, He stopped and stood to address the leaders so adamantly demanding a response. Suddenly, she felt like she was no longer the one on trial here but instead, this man, looking deep and lovingly into her eyes.

"If any one of you is without sin, let him be the first to throw a stone at her," He said, and then stooping down again, he continued His words in the dust. All around her it felt as if the wind had been sucked out of the room. After all the blustering and demands for a response, a verdict had been reached. No one made a move. Minutes passed as the religious leaders shifted uncomfortably in their stance. They looked at each other quickly and then down, the first to leave among the oldest, quietly slipping through the Temple doors and back out on to the street.

When all the accusers were gone, Jesus once again stood up, but this time He was directing His words to her. With a penetrating stare, He asked her who was left to condemn her. She searched the room and found no one there from the unforgiving mob that had seemed so bent on her destruction. "Neither do I," He spoke gently, "Go and sin no more," and the words found a new depth in her heart, her body resonating with a love and acceptance she had never known before.

She began to sob quietly into her hands, the tears flowing hard and fast down her cheeks as she whispered words of thankfulness to this figure of unconditional love. She had become the embodiment of a new Law, the Law of Love, and a living example of the Gospel. Because Jesus had not entered this world "to condemn the world, but to save the world through Him" *(John 3:17)*. And saved her He had. He saved her and chose her from before the creation of the world to be for generations, a blessed symbol of His mercy.

7

Neal's Story

By Neal Rozema

I've prayed for many years, wondering when the time would come that I would have enough strength and courage to tell the story of how Jesus Christ saved me from the grip of death and certain destruction. This story is for the lost, for those battling addiction, for the abused, and for those who feel empty, desperately seeking the one thing that can fill the void in their lives. Many have chosen drugs, alcohol, pornography, adulterous relationships, careers or whatever the enemy could throw at them to fill that big empty hole that can only be filled by the grace and love of Jesus Christ.

The power and the presence of Christ have been instilled in us since birth. Some people believe and diagnose this as our conscience, but where does our conscience come from? Even as children, Jesus warns us that what we are doing could cause harm, affecting ourselves or others in a negative way. It is the ultimate love. Atheists who claim not to believe in God or Jesus Christ, in their most desperate hour cry out, "God why have you allowed this!" Regardless of what you believe as a child or as an adult, when we are pushed to the brink, the one name that is always on everyone's lips is God. Our souls, created by God, will forever be tied in to His influence, His direction, and His love. That's the gift. His love is without end, calling to us from the very beginning. I have been commanded by Jesus Christ to share this story with all who will listen.

I grew up in a very broken and abusive home. From as early as I can remember, our family moved from state to state either running from the police, who were chasing my father, or visiting my father in whatever penitentiary he had landed in. My mother struggled to care for us, all the while trying to create a positive image of my father for her boys. We lived off food stamps, church charity, or other family members that would step in and help when they could.

As a child, I can still remember being tormented by demons and dark spirits. My bed would shake violently and the blankets would be ripped off while I slept. It was an ongoing conversation in my family about how the demonic forces seemed to follow us every time we moved. Doors would slam shut by themselves and voices would yell from other rooms. Unseen forces would even try to push us down the stairs. Two of my brothers died young and with tragic circumstances. I was tortured and relentlessly pursued by Satan and lived in constant fear every day. I never knew that through Christ I had the power and authority in His name to stop it.

My siblings and I were raised to be thieves, stealing for what we wanted and for what the family needed to survive. All who fell under the umbrella of my mother and father's influence saw the inside of a prison. I was first arrested at the age of sixteen for fraud, with many more arrests to follow. I was kicked out of numerous schools throughout my teen years for anger, fighting, skipping school, and so on. I was angry at everyone, knowing what I was doing was wrong, but desperately wanting the love and acceptance of my family and my father. My life became empty and tormented and I eventually filled that big, empty hole of mine with a severe heroin addiction.

I was given my first ten year sentence with the Illinois Department of Corrections at the age of twenty for a rash of burglaries to support my addiction. During that first incarceration, I lived in some of the deepest, darkest holes the state had to offer. Places where I watched an inmate commit suicide, not able to complete even a sixty day sentence. People were beaten and abused, just for pure entertainment. I fought to survive and learned to trust my instincts. At the end of that incarceration, I felt like I could still handle my life on my own. More than ever I was in control, but this time, I would be smarter. However, I quickly fell into old patterns. I was lost again, running from my addiction and the law. Many days and nights I contemplated suicide, because I knew the end result of where I was headed would be death.

The day came when the Lord's mercy had me arrested again, stealing to support my drug addiction. After being processed through the County Jail, I was led to where I would stay until trial. My first phone call was to my mother. Her response was to tell me to never call her again and that I was no longer a part of the family. She told me that I was nothing but an embarrassment and a disgrace. My next call was to my fiancé, who knew absolutely nothing about my criminal history or my drug addiction. Carrie was a born again Christian and had brought me to church with her a few times. She was the first person that could ever express the love of God to me and how important it was for my life. She answered the phone and started to tell me about how she found out that I was stealing and had a heroin addiction. Carrie fought back the tears of heartbreak and disappointment as she told me to never call her again.

For the first time in my life I was truly alone. I had lost everything that I cherished or loved. I hung up the phone and just stood there in complete shock and disappointment to what my life had become. A voice came over the loudspeakers telling all inmates to lock up. It took every ounce of my being to make it inside of that jail cell. When that door slammed, reality came crashing down. I cried uncontrollably, finally understanding what the direction and the choices of my life had brought me.

In my most desperate moment, at absolute rock bottom, I looked up and spoke to God for the first time. Having lost everything I said, "God, if You'll stand by me, if You will stay with me and protect me, I will follow You for the rest of my life." Then it happened! I collapsed on the floor absolutely motionless. I couldn't move; I couldn't see, but I could feel what was going on around me. I could feel the power and presence of God and the warmth of hands in my chest moving around inside of my body. The only way to describe the feeling was like He was removing things from inside me and replacing them with different things. Even though I was locked up in a jail cell, I could feel a breeze move over my body as things shifted and moved inside of me. The smell was clean and crisp, unlike anything I had ever encountered. Electricity and heat took over my body as I could feel the presence of something moving around me. What seemed like a lifetime was over in an instant.

My eyes opened and my energy spent, it took all that I had to get up onto the slab that was to be my bed. I instantly blacked out and found myself pinned down by a force that I could not see. I was suddenly in a rocky and desolate place where the clouds hung dark and fierce. I tried to move to get up, but I could not overpower the force that was pressing me down. In an instant, the clouds separated as the light shined down on a vision that I will never forget. It was the crucifixion, three crosses with Jesus in the middle.

As the Roman soldiers heckled and tormented Jesus, laughing at His pain and suffering, I fought with every ounce of my being to try to get up and intervene. I saw His mother, His disciples, crying and begging for mercy as they were pushed around by Roman soldiers. The soldiers sang songs and ridiculed Jesus as His family was made to watch. I fought, crying, and tried to yell out but my voice was completely inaudible. Held down, I watched the last minutes of Christ's sacrifice. Even now it brings me to tears remembering when His eyes shut and His head fell. Everything went dark, the earth shook and the wind roared over my body. Then the voice of God echoed, "Now…what will you do for Me?"

That moment, things inside of me changed. When I woke up, I could instantly feel the difference of God's grace. As time went on, I lost the desire to steal, to lie, or to depend on anything other than Jesus Christ. I had developed desperation for Jesus that was unquenchable. Sin's power was broken in me.

> *What shall we say, then? Shall we go on sinning so that grace may increase? By no means! We died to sin; how can we live in it any longer? Or don't you know that all of us who were baptized into Christ Jesus were baptized into his death? We were therefore buried with him through baptism into death in order that, just as Christ was raised from the dead through the glory of the Father, we too may live a new life.*
>
> *Romans 6:1-4*

God had given me a new spirit, and a new more purpose driven life. Days passed and I could feel the difference of what God had done. The anger and depression I had always carried with me were gone. The officer on duty called over the speakers telling me that I had a visitor. Knowing that everyone I loved had left me, I truly didn't know who this visitor could be. As I walked into that visiting room I saw the face of my fiancé, who to this day is now my wife. The first words out of her mouth were that she would wait for me. And that she did. Eight months later the judge handed down a ten year sentence, stating that due to my past arrests and prior convictions, I was "beyond rehabilitation". My wife and I served the ten year sentence that was given by the judge and faithfully, God kept His word. Not only was He with me every day, but He gifted me with the companionship of my wife.

8

Levi, also called Matthew

*Once again Jesus went out beside the lake.
A large crowd came to him, and he began to
teach them. As he walked along, he saw Levi
son of Alphaeus sitting at the tax collector's
booth. "Follow me," Jesus told him, and
Levi got up and followed him.*

Mark 2:13-14

The sun was hot that day, beating down on his
coarse black hair, beads of sweat trickling slowly
down his neck. Levi cursed to himself; he hated
this post, this assignment somewhere between
Damascus and the seaports of Phoenicia. He had
been stationed off this dusty road by the chief tax
collector for the office of "receipt of custom". Worn
and weary travelers entering this Roman territory
would have to pay a tax on their goods and
possessions and this man, Levi, was there to collect.

A tax collector was not what Levi had wanted
for himself as a boy. In fact, he had often sworn that

he would never follow in the footsteps of his father, Alphaeus, extorting his fellow Jews to fatten his own wallet. His father paid a terrible price. Despised and rejected by his countrymen and in league with a Rome that cared only for what he could collect for them, he turned to drinking away his shame, spending late nights in taverns with fellow thieves and prostitutes.

Often times his father would come home too drunk to stand and beat anyone who got in his way. That was usually Levi's mother but sometimes his children would catch the brunt of his violence with marks to show for it for days. Levi hated him, fear driving him into the corners of his home during his father's drunken tirades, begging God in the dark to rid their family of this disease. But it continued to happen night after night until his father, attempting to fight off the emptiness that was swallowing him whole, found comfort in the arms of another woman and abandoned their small family altogether.

It was a relief when his father left, however, it was momentary. With all the loss of income, the family had quickly fallen into starvation. Suddenly destitute, Levi and his siblings went to the streets to try to feed the family. The boys began stealing from local vendors or passer-bys in the crowd; and his sister told to make money however she could, sold the only thing she had of any value, herself.

Levi was angry and desperate. So when he was introduced to the chief tax collector of their territory and told he could make a lot of money working for Rome, he decided that maybe he could walk the path his father had taken, especially if it meant he might get his sister off the street, his mother a fine place to live.

He accepted the offer and began his work, taking his anger out on his fellow Jews. He would take what so many had been unwilling to give when his family had been most desperate. He would take that and a lot more for the bad luck he had been given. He mercilessly extorted money from everyone around him, cursing their hatred and drowning himself at night at the local taverns with people that accepted him and called him friend.

From his post, Levi saw Jesus coming from quite a distance, throngs of people in His wake. Many faces familiar to him formed the crowd. He had heard of this Rabbi before, in fact, everyone he knew was talking about Him, this miracle working teacher of the law and "friend of sinners". He laughed out loud when told that this was a different kind of teacher; that He seemed to welcome the outcasts of society to come and listen, even eating with other tax collectors, a sign of friendship that no Jew had ever seen from a teacher of religious law. This man must be looking for trouble, Levi thought, and He was guaranteed to find it, remembering the haughty eyes and disdain he had felt at the hands of the Pharisees.

But His boldness intrigued Levi; this teacher seemed a man not unlike himself. A man who was determined, resilient and unafraid to consort with those so many people considered scum. Perhaps this teacher was able to see in them what Levi had so often seen, the pain of broken promises and the tired eyes of sorrow heaped on sorrow. Levi had grown to love these people, an adopted family held together by torment.

Levi strained from his post to try to get a better look at this man, Jesus, coming poised to pass directly in front of him. He waited, anticipation growing, to see this One so famous for being a friend to tax collectors. Could it be true? Would he find friendship instead of scowling eyes from this teacher of God?

Coming closer, Levi could see this Jesus didn't appear much different from any other Jew he would often come into contact with. There was nothing in His appearance that would cause anyone to be attracted to Him. It was only in His countenance that Levi perceived a difference from the other religious leaders of the day. His eyes seemed to twinkle and sparkle with love and his laugh indicated a true friendship with those around Him. Jesus seemed to genuinely delight in their company, even with the sweat, dust and frazzled nerves of a crowd desperate to be close to Him.

Levi had been taking in the scene for a while now, sitting in his booth, trying desperately to relieve himself of the squelching heat. Dropping his makeshift fan, he bent over, cursing, to pick it up, only to rise again and find himself face to face with Jesus. His mouth, opened slightly in surprise, quickly shut as he suddenly had no words to offer this bold Rabbi.

Jesus looked down at him, a smile playing across His lips, "Come, be My disciple," He said with intensity and purpose. Levi gave a start, a *disciple*? Didn't this man know who he was? He was a thief, a swindler. Surely this man must know all the sins that could be counted against him. His life had not been like other Jewish boys. He was never expected to continue on in school, never even taught a trade. Certainly he was never expected to attend the beth midrash to learn under the rabbi a deeper meaning of the Torah. Yet Jesus was asking him to be His *talmidim*, a disciple, to spend his days and nights learning everything he could about Himself. The talmidim were special, the best of the best, and Levi knew he was not, only a tax collector and drunk like his father before him.

But this Jesus remained steadfast, staring deep into Levi's eyes, penetrating his heart and beckoning him forward, calling him to higher ground. Without further thought, Levi jumped to his feet, scrambled out of his post and followed Him down the dusty road, leaving everything he had of value behind.

Later, Levi would invite Jesus to his home, preparing a great banquet in His honor. Jesus would come and break bread with the lowest of the low, or so they were perceived. When questioned why such a great teacher would lower himself to fellowship with such scum, Jesus replied with the light of love blazing in His eyes, "Healthy people don't need a doctor- sick people do. I have come to call not those who think they are righteous, but those who know they are sinners" (*Mark 2:17, NLT*). For Jesus knew what Levi would later see, as part of the King's inner circle, that "all have sinned and fall short of the glory of God" (*Romans 3:23*).

9

The Long Years

Ten years in the Illinois Department of Corrections...I felt like I had been punched in the stomach. How could someone receive ten years for stealing a wallet out of a gym locker? But the judge, no longer believing anything positive could come from Neal's life, opted to send him away to help society if only by getting him off the streets. I was devastated and Neal, allowing himself to be led, shackled and by armed guards to the side door of the courtroom, barely looked up to say goodbye.

I sat in my car in the covered parking lot of the courthouse and cried. Neal was going to prison for a while. He would be eligible for parole after five years and if he worked hard and kept his head down, he may be able to get six months off for "good behavior". But that still meant Neal would be away for four and a half years. Neal told me he could handle prison. He had done it before and could do it again if he had to. He assuaged my fears by assuring me he could fight; he would be smart and everything would be okay. I believed him and took some comfort but still the knot that had formed in the pit of my stomach would not be undone. So much could happen in four and a half years.

Then there was me. I was 27 years old and would be turning 31 days after he was projected to come home. These were prime years if I was going to remarry or have any children. What if I waited all that time, only to have it all fall apart again? All these thoughts raced through my head and it felt like maybe God had abandoned us. The punishment felt so severe and yet deep inside I felt He was still there and had a plan.

It was a few months earlier, while I sat praying in my mother's loft, staring absently out of the second story window, that the Lord had asked me the question, *Do you trust Me?* Suddenly, I was paying attention. "Yes, Lord, I trust You," I replied. *Would I lie to you, Carrie?* He asked again. "No, Lord, never," I spoke adamantly from my heart. *Then put your ring back on,* He said.

It was in the midst of all the revelations about Neal, I had quietly slipped off my engagement ring, placing it safely in my top dresser drawer. And even after the Lord had instructed me to stand by Neal, to pray and intercede, I was still unsure if all this would lead to marriage. *You will have to make your intentions very plain, Lord, if you want me to put the ring back on*, I had spoken to Him in prayer, several times over. So after months of weekly visits to County Jail, collect calls and lengthy letters, the

Lord made Himself plain. I jumped to my feet, ran to my dresser and hastily put the ring back on. I was overjoyed to be engaged to him again. To me it was an unspoken promise that we were going to overcome all of this and that what I believed the Lord had been saying to me throughout our courtship was indeed true. Looking down at my hand, I was thrilled. Then, as minutes passed, I began to feel the weight of the cross the Lord had just asked me to carry.

Almost everyone close to me was aware of the circumstances surrounding Neal and I. Everyone had breathed a big sigh of relief that I discovered the truth in time. And most nodded hesitant approval at my attempts to help and support Neal through his crisis, as a friend. But wearing his ring would be an entirely different matter. It was a symbol to the world that I believed we would be together forever. A statement of faith so shocking that most would be forced to believe that somewhere in this process, Carrie had lost her mind. Or at best, Carrie was a very confused and damaged girl that couldn't see how many other more appealing options were out there for her.

Regardless of how I felt certain to be perceived, neither line of thinking would be very complimentary to my character. I would have to be brave, swallow my pride and completely trust God. So when the judge told Neal ten years, I knew he also meant me, and that we would be doing every bit of that time together.

Like a man returning from war, Neal had very rarely talked about what his life had been like the first time he had hit the Illinois Department of

Corrections. Only a few stories here and there but it was enough to know that where he was going was the closest thing to hell on earth.

The first time I saw Neal after being transferred to Danville Correctional Center, my heart sank to the floor. It had been close to six weeks since I had last seen him at the courthouse and his appearance was changed dramatically. Pale skin and sunken eyes told me he wasn't sleeping well. He had traded in his orange county jumpsuit for navy blues and his clothes hung loosely from his now thin frame. We held hands at a table for four, chairs bolted to the floor, nestled deep in a sea of institutional grey. Mothers, girlfriends, wives, and children surrounded us, each one tending to their inmate, but Neal and I remained locked in each other's gaze, reveling in the fact we were able to touch again after almost a year of glass partitions.

I was ecstatic to see him but the depths of his depression were all over his face. "I am a number again...K61197," he said, looking at the guard, then the floor and slowly back up to me. An officer sat mean and heavy at the end of the room, pencil in hand, ready to pounce if ever any of us got out of line. I squeezed his hand tighter, "Not to me," I replied, attempting in vain to lift his spirits.

That first day, I stayed for hours, searching for words but finding there was little that could be said. Taking comfort in each other's presence, we held hands as if holding on to life, fingers locked, feeding each other hope that one day this would all be over and a memory. Driving back from Danville, I sobbed nearly the whole way. This was not going to be easy but this was to be the way of things for a while.

Life had stopped for Neal in the confines of his cell, but my life had to go on. I went home and went to work as a caseworker for foster care on the south side of Chicago. I traveled the inner city and saw firsthand the devastation wrought by drugs, violence and forgotten children. To renew my hope, I attended Moody Bible Institute in the evenings, studying Urban Ministry. If God was able to heal us, He was certainly able to heal other homes, neighborhoods, cities, indeed the world. All the while, I made weekend runs to visit Neal as often as I could. I lost friends. People I had known for years suddenly stopped calling. I held tighter to the Lord's hand and trusted Him for friendships.

I drove a lot in those days, listening to Christian radio, blasting songs of praise to lift my spirit when I would get discouraged. I listened to the five point plans of famous preachers on how to make sure you were marrying God's perfect mate and laughed to myself. Neal always failed on every point but still I looked to heaven as the Lord encouraged me on, clearly not dissuaded.

I was on fire for our testimony in the early days, telling anyone who would listen about what God was doing in our lives. Sharing our story at a homeless shelter in downtown Chicago, the room had erupted in praise, grown men moved to tears to hear the call of God on us. However, most people would listen with thinly veiled skepticism, which bothered me but also added fuel to the fire. I was standing with the cross, preaching a Gospel that most couldn't believe.

I would spend evenings in the Word, listening to the melodic sounds of Ginny Owens singing:

*Beneath the symbol of a lost cause is where I
take my stand,
Beneath the emblem of a Roman cross and of a
sacrificial lamb.
Cause love never claims the victory till it finally
gives it's all,
And that's why the grave is empty, beneath the
symbol of a lost cause.*

Ginny Owens, *Ginny Owens*
"Symbol of a Lost Cause"

To most, my love was a lost cause but to my Jesus, he was clay in His hands. Why could no one see how amazing this was? For most people it was just too impossible to believe and it wasn't that I couldn't understand why. It was just that God had so filled me with faith, that I shook my fist in the face of it and pressed on.

All the while, we stayed close, writing five page letters several days a week, making collect calls until I couldn't afford it, and visiting each other as often as possible. We spent every holiday, birthday and anniversary within the sterile walls of a distant and forsaken visiting room. Spring turned to summer, to winter, to fall and all the seasons saw my now blue Chevy Cavalier driving miles and miles for love. We were a cord of three strands, Jesus, Neal and I, not easily broken while the words of the King resonated in my heart, "Greater love has no one than this, that he lay down his life for his friends" (*John 15:13*).

I kept praying, repeating with fervency the intercessory prayers my friend had provided for me.

When Neal had been away for a couple of years, I started to notice something strange happening late at night while I was sleeping in my bed. It was a gentle and persistent shake that would inevitably wake me up from sleep. I was under demonic attack. Neal had grown up with demons visiting him at night, slapping his feet, shaking his bed and ripping off his covers while he slept, but this was my very first experience with such an aggressive attack.

It persisted for months and I prayed fervently for it to stop. I never really felt fear over the intrusion; more anger that this spirit believed it could now harass me. I spoke to pastors and read as many books as I could to figure out how to make it all end. Not until I picked up a book discussing generational curses and prayers to break them, sending it in for Neal to pray, did the shaking finally stop.

That is not to say there was no longer attack. One day I had taken a client of mine to a food pantry to pick up some items, only to be accosted by a women sneering at me from the corner. Looking at me with dark eyes, she made a beeline to me in a room full of people, and attempted to push me around the room. I was so new to spiritual warfare at this point that the enemy successfully bullied me out of the door and for months I worried over it. I was praying very direct, visceral prayers that whatever forces that had been robbing Neal of life and the life of his family would now have to leave and the enemy was clearly unhappy about it. But God filled me with so much faith; I persisted in prayers, believing that certainly Neal's life was worth any attempts of the enemy to discourage me.

Neal rarely told me what was going on, always preferring to talk about me, my life, and our relationship. He was changing, though, I could see. I sent him every self-help spiritual book known to man and we talked about all the things of God. The Lord faithfully used the time for us to dig out so much of the dirt and corruption of our past. We worked through things together and we became stronger. I read a lot and avoided any environment that might get me in trouble. Neal attended services inside, learned how to tell the truth and what love really looked like.

It was a nightmare and it was healing, a necessary torture as God began to lay the foundation and framework for a real relationship. What seemed like punishment was more like mercy; we had been doomed to failure and He was rescuing us. The Lord was so exceedingly generous with faith, filling us up in our lowest moments and giving us peace in the storms. With the gentle command to marry this man, the Lord poured out His Spirit into me so completely that I felt able to overcome anything. He had given me a promise and a hope for Neal that my love and his, wrapped in the love of the Father would be more than sufficient to tear down every obstacle in our path. Nothing would be impossible for us. He whispered this promise into my heart:

"For I know the plans I have for you," declares the Lord, "Plans to prosper you and not to harm you, plans to give you a hope and a future."

Jeremiah 29:11

This truly was the Gospel, the reason Christ had come to this earth, died and rose again. He was able to defeat all the power of the enemy, so that in our moments of intense darkness, His light would shine, healing and transforming us from the inside out. If Neal and I could not be fully restored than what were we all talking, singing and praying about in church? A new fire burned steadily in me, day by day, that the Good News of the Gospel was real, relevant and able to do more than I could possibly imagine.

Neal would move several times over the next few years, sometimes to better, easier institutions with more freedom and privileges, and sometimes to worse places. We navigated a system that at times seemed so impossible to overcome. Two steps forward, three steps back, we danced our way through the myriad of rules and procedures that each new institution offered.

After so many years, we grew tired. I faced constant scrutiny for my relationship with Neal and as the time approached for him to come home, the opposition intensified. Many well-meaning friends at church tried to dissuade me from making any long term plans with Neal. They insisted he be made to get on his feet and prove himself before any commitment was made. I kept insisting that God had told me to marry him and it seemed so ironic to me that I was fighting Christians to try to accomplish what the Lord had clearly told me to do. Neal had abandoned every family member and every friend to follow Christ and had no one in the world now but me. Although their advice was reasonable, it would have been disobedient to the Lord, a step of fear and not of faith.

As the pressure mounted, I knew I would be forced to look for a new church home. This couldn't be Neal's first experience with the family of God, people with their arms crossed waiting for Neal to "prove" himself. I wanted him to come home and feel all the love Christ had for him, to be welcomed with open arms and by people that believed he would overcome.

The Lord led me to a small church not far from my home that seemed a perfect fit. Attendees with tattoos and backgrounds similar to Neal warmly welcomed me at the door. I told our story and it was received without the usual look of fear I had grown accustomed to at church. Grateful to finally feel comfortable with a church family, we began to look forward in anticipation to his homecoming. We had fought hard; he, to survive the unrelenting chaos of prison and me, to hold off the pressure of a world that just couldn't believe this was God's will. So in the final days, we held on with both hands to the impenetrable hope that sustained us for so long, and fell, exhausted on our knees across the finish line.

10

The Samaritan Woman of the Well

When a Samaritan woman came to draw water, Jesus said to her, "Will you give me a drink?" (His disciples had gone into the town to buy food). The Samaritan woman said to him, "You are a Jew and I am a Samaritan woman. How can you ask me for a drink?" (For Jews do not associate with Samaritans). Jesus answered her, "If you knew the gift of God and who it is that asks you for a drink, you would have asked him and he would have given you living water."

John 4:7-10

The Samaritan woman squinted up at the sky, a jar for water at her hip, and began her arduous climb to the well. The sun was high and hot that day and she felt the heat pelting her head and shoulders through the layers of cloth wrapped around her. She knew the ladies of the village would only draw water in the morning and evening hours so, watching out her window until she was sure it was noon, she waited for the middle of the day to be absolutely certain of no company. For many years the Father had watched her make this climb, alone and suffering under her layers of clothing. He heard her sobs at night for One who could redeem her from what her life had become. She had been calling out for a Savior for a long time, only she had mistaken Him over and over again.

She was only a child when she had placed all her hope and faith in a man who was not able to return the adoration. Satan had whispered in his ear years before that he could not be loved, so with both fists he attempted to shut out any attempts to show him otherwise. He could beat the love out of anyone and would do it over and over again, until the words were silenced, with all the remains of love left whimpering in a corner. So it had not come as a surprise when one evening he had not returned home, the victim of a knife in the shadows of the village, retribution from a stranger strong enough to fight back.

She went to live with his brother then, an attempt to carry on his name having been childless at his death. It was there she understood the curse of generations and that it was not only one brother who could hit, but two, having grown up with it themselves at the hands of their father. But that was not the full extent of her abuse as the other women of the home, having no appreciation for the newly acquired competition, made her life a living hell by keeping his wrath pointed at her for things she had never done.

It was here that she began to entertain thoughts of running away, making her ripe for a young, adventurous husband number three to sweep her off her feet, promising her a new life outside the village and far away from all her enemies. However, they had only gotten as far as the next town over before he had a change of plans, opting for a more lucrative opportunity with a woman of means to help him pursue all the desires of his heart.

Broken and cast out, she returned in shame, taking refuge in the home of a widow who tolerated her presence only for the sake of a little company. She would have to work though, a woman with little skills, and would be taken in as help at one of the local establishments, a refuge for travelers and those with scandal on their mind.

The owner pursued her persistently and she tolerated his advances for the sake of work, but when a fast talking peddler of wares had stopped in for a drink, she thought again she saw a way out. She gathered her belongings, believing the soft words of love he had spoken in the moonlight, and married him in hopes to tie him to all his empty promises. But it had done little more than delay his inevitable departure without her; his only desire to secure a woman in every town to ease the loneliness of many travels.

The fifth husband was the worst, stealing her money and leaving town with any last hope of salvation she had. So throwing her hands up in despair, she believed the enemy's lies that said she was worth nothing, incapable of love and unworthy to receive it. She retreated further and further into her shell, hardening her heart to such a place that she would try to convince herself she could no longer feel the pain, that it no longer mattered. But somewhere, somehow it must still because every day she waited, letting the hours slowly pass until she felt certain to be alone, fetching water at the well.

It wasn't that she hated the company of the other women. Some of them could even feign kindness and make polite conversation. She would listen to them prattle on about their husbands and children, their plans for the holidays, their goings on in the village. She would listen and know she would never be invited over for dinner, never be a part of their social groups, and never know what it was like to be one of them. It wasn't an overt offensive attack, although there were some that couldn't hide their disdain at her present circumstances, living with a man that refused to marry her. It was the more subtle way they excluded her, quietly reminding her that she would never be as good as them.

The Father had seen every one of her tears, the broken dreams and constant search for a great love to rescue her from her deplorable circumstances. She called out to Him for deliverance and today, He was sending His Son. Head down she climbed faithfully to the edge of the well and began to draw the water, where Jesus, who was resting wearily yet in anticipation for this moment, happily told her the Savior had come. He told her that and so much more, not in spite of all that had happened to her but because of it. He knew if anyone needed a Messiah, it was her, and His love for her would penetrate so deep that nothing and no one would be able to stop her from professing it.

Upon hearing the message, the Samaritan woman raced back to her village with her heart pounding in her chest, her jar of water still resting at the well. He knew everything about her but had not treated her like the poison she felt herself to be. Instead He spoke with a love and tenderness she had never known before. She had to know if it could be true, had her Savior finally come?

This was why she was now compelled, contrary to all her inclinations of the past to hide, to go back to her village and share this Good News with the others. She was now an instrument of righteousness to herald a coming King, using the shame of her story to bring salvation to many.

And because of her testimony, Jesus would remain two more days, revealing life to the people of Sychar. The despised, rejected Samaritan believers would be among the first to believe, receiving the message from one of the most broken of their own. Their desperation caused their hearts to open like a flower before Him, a fragrance the King fully loved. For in Samaria and for years to come, this was how the kingdom of God would often work, pouring out the Father's love on the most broken, wielding power in humility and laying its foundation on the scattered ashes of broken dreams.

11

New Beginnings

I woke up early in a dark, cold hotel room waiting for first light. This was the day Neal was coming home and I had barely slept the night before. Rolling over to the nightstand, I picked up my Bible to invite some calm to my heart. It was hard to believe after being apart for four and a half years, this day had finally come. The Lord led me to Galatians 5:1, "It is for freedom that Christ has set us free. Stand firm, then, and do not let yourselves be burdened again by a yoke of slavery." So with a commitment to freedom in my heart, I put on the linen dress I bought for the occasion, took one last look in the mirror to smooth my reflection and drove the half mile down the road to meet Neal.

We drove for miles that day in a blazing August heat, holding hands and stealing kisses as the car roared on into a new future. I could see Neal struggling to reorient himself to life outside the walls he had grown so accustomed to, smiling up at me and then staring thoughtfully out his window. It was all so surreal, as if in a moment we could be back holding hands across a hard, institutional table. It felt so much like a dream. We drove on as every mile allowed a little more reality to sink in.

Nobody was excited about this day, nobody except us. We knew God had told us that we were to be married but there were no wedding plans, no money for elaborate flowers and covered chairs, and no smiling faces to bless our future. So ten days after faithfully picking him up at the correctional center, Neal and I married before the Justice of the Peace.

It was one of the most beautiful days of my life as Neal and I sat holding hands in a sea of faces. Some in our company looked like they were about to be sentenced to life, while others were clearly enjoying the spontaneity of the moment. For Neal and me, it was pure joy. My spirit was light and airy as we walked up to the podium to say our vows, a happy photographer snapping pictures from my camera, later reflecting bright, angelic balls of light surrounding us as we pledged our love. The peace in the room was palpable, heavenly and full of promise. Ten dollars, ten minutes and everything we had worked so hard for had arrived. Now as newlyweds we felt ready to face all the trouble life was about to throw our way.

Newly released from prison, Neal struggled to find a job. Having a criminal record and being honest about it made it extremely difficult for him to find employment that could pay the bills. He started back at square one, working in a local

71

restaurant chain that was willing to take the risk of hiring an ex-con. He worked seven days a week, and with as many shifts as he could so that we could make enough money to start a family. Dragging himself there through the stomach flu, snow storms and in competition with people half his age, he worked tirelessly to provide for us. Through God's favor and provision, we made enough to pay the bills and became pregnant three months later.

It was a sweet and challenging time. Neal and I fought hard to keep our feet on solid ground and took on obstacles one step at a time. Eventually all of Neal's hard work paid off when his employer asked him to enter management. After interviewing with their human resources department, Neal was required to complete a background check for the first time. We paced for weeks not knowing what the outcome would be. Neal had told them that he had a criminal history but it was much different to see the extent of it on paper.

I dropped him off at nine-o-clock in the morning to continue his management training only to receive a phone call from Neal thirty minutes later that I needed to come pick him up. With tears in his eyes, he told me the details of his criminal record had not only stopped him from getting a management job, but also cost him the job he had as a server.

As management had informed him of his release, Neal's first thought was, *"What do I tell my wife?"* But just as quickly as fear crept in, a peace suddenly came over him. He told his supervisors what an honor and privilege it had been to work for them as long as he had to support his family. He shook everyone's hand and thanked them, knowing in that moment that God had something better for all of us. The Lord, in His infinite wisdom, knew Neal's loyalty would have kept him there forever and He had other plans.

My heart broke for him but midterm in my pregnancy; we knew that God would take care of us. We had come too far to go out like this. Days passed of filling out applications, and being rejected again and again for his criminal background. Finally his journey brought him to a restaurant that didn't ask the infamous question: *Have you ever been convicted of a felony*? Careful to project to the general manager the determination he had to support his family and make their restaurant the very best it could be, he was hired on the spot and made three times what he had made at his previous employment.

With God's favor this was just the beginning. This restaurant was owned and operated by billionaires and throughout Neal's tenure there, he developed a strong relationship with the owners. It wasn't long before Neal was promoted to bar manager. God had raised Neal from a criminal to one of the most respected people in his industry. He had transformed Neal from a thief to managing millions of dollars. With all the blessing and favor of the Lord upon him, people were drawn to Neal and loved being in his presence. Without Jesus he would have been their worst nightmare. But in Christ, he was accomplishing things that nobody would ever have believed.

Many nights Neal stood looking out over the crowd in the restaurant in utter amazement at what was possible through Jesus Christ. In those moments, he could see God holding his soul like a trophy in front of all of hell, saying, "*You thought you had him, but Neal is mine.*"

Slowly we were building our small family. Just prior to the birth of our first son, we moved to a two bedroom apartment in our complex. It was a piece of heaven for us and we quickly went about decorating the baby's room in anticipation for his arrival. By keeping our expenses low, I was able to quit my job and be a full time mom. For me, it was a dream come true. We climbed further and further out of the hole we had started in, making progress every day and finding new hope around every corner.

We kept our eyes on Jesus but still Satan kept after us, throwing every temptation in our path to try to cause a young marriage to stumble. We struggled in our new church as it suffered from a lack of accountability. We felt led to quietly leave the church after months of prayer. So many years in the Department of Corrections had taught us that we could trust each other and the Lord would show us the best way, always faithful to pick us up when we blew it and encourage us in faith when we struggled.

When the enemy couldn't trip us up with the stresses of life, he attempted more aggressive attacks. One night, Neal was held down for several minutes struggling under a dark spirit. When I arrived home, it had left, but Neal was clearly shaken. Through prayer we took more proactive steps in keeping the enemy out of our house by praying over every door frame and commanding all the powers of darkness away from our small family.

After working a couple of years at the restaurant, a regular at his establishment, looking for some good tenants, offered to rent us a home for nearly the same price we were paying for our apartment. We drove by the property and our mouths dropped open in shock. It was a beautiful home nestled among rows of tall pine trees, a bright red barn in the back to accent an already picturesque view. God was moving us into a home of our dreams and we were in complete awe.

But after only a few weeks in our new home, we would have to face the enemy again. Night after night, I was filled with a feeling of dread that I couldn't explain. Again, I would wake up with our bed shaking, a more violent outburst from the enemy than I had experienced before. After investigating several unspiritual possibilities and following a morning where I truly believed we must have experienced an earthquake, only to find the news quiet about any such event, Neal and I clasped hands to command any evil spirit out of the home.

That evening while Neal was away at work, I sat praying on my knees in the middle of the living room. Suddenly, a loud thud shook the floor beneath me as if someone had just punched the floor boards underneath. My dog, who had been on her back in front of me, quickly flipped over and began barking hysterically. The Holy Spirit moved in my heart and all the years I had spent praying intercession for Neal quickly kicked in. I began to walk through the house, commanding all evil to leave in the mighty name of Jesus. I walked down into the basement with righteous anger to pray the enemy out of every corner of our home. This continued for approximately twenty minutes until the Holy Spirit flooded me with peace that the spirit was gone, and I knew it was time to stop praying. From that night on, our bed never shook again and all feelings of fear and dread were gone. Praise God!

After living in our home only a few short months, the walls around our family began to shake again as the details of Neal's criminal past came around front and center at his work. A background check had been done and word had gotten back to the owners. The air around him changed and their trust was gone. Moving on would be inevitable; everything he did now scrutinized to the finest detail.

We prayed and trusted God for better. Leaving his position, he found work at another restaurant close by, which helped to pay the bills but could not fully cover the standard of living we had acquired. I watched little ones to stay home with mine. Yet we felt blessed during this time, watching God provide for us in new and unimaginable ways while benefiting from the generosity of friends and family who had grown to accept and even cheer for us.

We made it through and learned that God was fully able to meet all our needs and that He would always provide. Our world was shaking but God's perfect will was being done. With a child at home, Neal prayed for a career that would allow him to spend his nights with us, away from all the perils of working in a bar. It had been a way to get on our feet but no place, he felt, for a family man.

While in prison, Neal attended college classes, one of which was a two year degree in horticulture. The house we had moved into and our current landlord was also the owner of one of the most successful landscaping companies in Illinois. Neal took a step of faith, asking our new landlord if he might be able to pick up hours doing odd jobs around the property, to which he heartily agreed. He knew nothing of Neal's credentials, his experience, or his background and yet he still wanted Neal to work for him, offering a full time position as a project and crew manager for the company months later when his horticulture studies came to light. Neal would be helping to manage a multimillion dollar business that employed over 200 people.

How great is God! His mercies and His favor had Neal in a brand new career, able to support his family with virtually no experience. The power of God was beyond the limitations and reasoning of human resources and the business world. It was beyond the limitations of credentials and experience. God had overcome all that the world had said was garbage and "beyond rehabilitation".

We began a long and arduous journey to find a church home where we felt loved and accepted. We tried so many on for size and struggled to find a fit. We shared our testimony with a few churches and experienced rejection. Our story wasn't a clean one or free of sin. Many were uncomfortable that God would call a young girl to marry a convict. Many didn't want to talk about demonic warfare in the sense we had experienced it. I began to wonder how people like Neal with severe demonic strongholds ever got free if people in church were not talking about warfare prayer and deliverance.

Most of the people we met were genuinely nice but knew nothing of the Department of Corrections. They had not been drug addicted or divorced. We were instantly relegated to support groups which was isolating in a sense, as if we were the damaged ones that belonged over there and didn't fit in with the others in the body of Christ. I learned how difficult it can be for those coming out of circumstances like ours to find a place in the family of God.

I learned that the current church model has a very distinct culture, a way of talking and interacting and unless you can play the part, you never quite fit in. I realized there were probably many more out there like us who had experienced God through the pain of life, who still had the marks and scars of the world on them that made it hard to assimilate well into the local church. Maybe we still swore. Maybe we had a lot of tattoos or dressed immodestly. Maybe we were single parents struggling to support a family. Maybe we had our defenses up from so much abuse, making it hard to walk into small groups and share our story. I knew from experience that even when salvation comes, change doesn't happen over night. My heart was burdened for "the least of these" and the ones who get lost because they feel like they don't fit.

However, despite our obstacles, Neal has remained abstinent from drugs and has passionately pursued Christ with all his heart. Our family has grown to two young boys, our bills have always been paid and God continues to demonstrate his love for our family on a daily basis, providing everything we need as we need it and navigating us around pitfalls to bring us peace.

Neal has been a voice to the lost and broken, the lonely souls that would often sit stranded at his bar. We know that God cherishes the broken even if we've often felt rejected at church; we have seen it and felt it intimately. God loves the ones he won back from the enemy, His Word forever in our hearts:

> *My son, do not forget my teaching, but keep my commands in your heart, for they will prolong your life many years and bring you prosperity.*
> *Let love and faithfulness never leave you; bind them around your neck, write them on the tablet of your heart.*
> *Then you will win favor and a good name in the sight of God and man.*
> *Trust in the Lord with all your heart and lean not on your own understanding; in all your ways acknowledge him, and he will make your paths straight.*
> *Do not be wise in your own eyes; fear the Lord and shun evil.*
> *This will bring health to your body and nourishment to your bones.*
> *Proverbs 3:1-8*

The power of Jesus is amazing. Only He could take the scraps of what Neal was and make him the man he is today. Only He could bring a divorced and bankrupt woman to a home full of children and love.

And yet it is not just our story, only an extension of what Jesus has been doing for so many for centuries. When we are in charge, we end up a mess, but when we surrender our lives to Jesus and allow Him to direct our paths, even though we often make mistakes, He brings us more than we could ever hope to imagine. This story is just a part of many miracles that the living Christ still performs to this day. It's all about Him! His glory, His grace and His favor have made us unrecognizable to those who knew us before. They stand in awe and wonder at the victory of our lives. So to all that will read this and to all that will listen- your hope lies in Jesus Christ; He is the only One who can save you.

12

Rahab, the Prostitute

Then Joshua son of Nun secretly sent two spies from Shittim. "Go, look over the land," he said, "especially Jericho." So they went and entered the house of a prostitute named Rahab and stayed there.

Joshua 2:1

Black smoke rising, thick and heavy above a pile of rocks and rubble, Rahab awoke, sitting straight up in bed, covered with sweat and clutching her chest. This was the third nightmare in the last week of her city, Jericho, fallen and smoldering, bodies strewn about her. Three nights where she awoke in a panic and now felt certain this was not a coincidence.

There had been so much talk in town of late of these Israelites and what the Lord their God had done, rescuing them from Egypt by drying up the Red Sea and completely destroying the Amorites east of the Jordan. As the Israelites had grown closer to their walls and seem poised to descend on them, the entire town was melting in fear.

Rahab had heard the stories over and over again, listening to the travelers pass in and out of her doors but had not thought much of it, her own life much more of a prison for her than any attacking army could threaten her with. What could they do to her that hadn't already been done? She had shrugged off the stories, muttering under her breath that seeing Jericho burn would be no great loss to her. Truth be told, she no longer cared if she lived or died, death a seeming relief from her day to day torment.

Life had not always been this way for Rahab. Growing up as a small child in her parents home, she had many fond memories of times spent with her mother in the garden, her father, a laborer, quietly slumbering in his chair at the end of a long day.

Her mother had been the one to tell her to pay attention to dreams. Rahab had often heard her mother spend hours in front of her gods, praying for help, when nightmares had awoken her from a fitful sleep. Omens, her mother believed, and so she had heard her mother cry late into the night, pleading with dark forces to be delivered of evil. Yet all her mother's pleas had been in vain, for dark forces eventually came for her family, tearing them apart.

Rahab was only nine when the enemy came to steal her innocence. Believing her favorite uncle had only good intentions, she had been surprised at the sudden attack. Pinned down by the weight of a man three times her size, her muffled screams for help went unanswered. She sat in dread upon news her uncle would be coming to visit often, knowing for certain he came with one purpose. She had wanted to tell her parents but the shame of it seemed too unbearable to confess. Sure it was her fault, tempting him in her playfulness, how could she now admit to this? It would break her parents' heart and life would never be the same. So the abuse continued for years until the age when Rahab could no longer bear the torment and tried to escape the prison of her home.

She met an older man when she was only thirteen, who said she was beautiful and had big plans for their future. He bought her expensive clothes and took her to special places to profess his love, her need to be loved causing her to quickly fall prey to his multitude of lies. She broke off with her family, her parents in torment and not understanding why their girl would want to run off with such a man.

She took up space with him, ready to start fresh in a new life. But by the third evening, Rahab, came face to face with the life this man had in mind. Being introduced to a "friend", her lover had quietly took her into the other room and assured her that her moments with this new gentlemen would be quick and the money so good they would be able to eat for a week. She cried, deep and heavy into his arm, but because she loved him, she made up her mind not to tell him no.

So it began, as he would bring men home for her to entertain, all her dreams of love and family went up in smoke. Each week became more progressively filled with empty promises and violence. She threatened to leave, but only once, as the beating she received was so severe she was in bed for days and felt certain that he would make good on his promises to kill her family if she ever managed an escape. So she stayed, enduring the hell that came with each new face and becoming what the men wanted to survive.

So when Rahab heard the Israelites were coming, she said to herself, "Let it burn..." and quietly prayed she would not be spared. Yet these recent nightmares had her gasping for air in the middle of the night, a small voice inside telling her that she did indeed want to live and avoid the destruction that was heading her way. It was then, in the early morning hours, Rahab rolled over onto her knees and prayed to the God of the Israelites that if He would spare her and her family that she would do anything He asked, serving Him only with all that was left of her.

And so when Rahab saw the young Israelite men at her door, seeking shelter and a place to hide, she knew instantly her prayers had been answered and what she must do. When the King of Jericho came looking for them, she hid the men on the roof and sent the soldiers away in hot pursuit the wrong direction, ensuring the Israelites would make it safely home.

At great risk to her life, she would protect these men in obedience to the God of the Israelites. In return, He would spare her life, offering her a freedom she had not dared to hope for before. The Israelite men agreed, telling her to bring her entire family into her home and by hanging a scarlet cord from her window, she would ensure they would all be spared.

The great love of a Father, who did not see her sins as she called out to Him, only a broken and bleeding heart that needed to be rescued and was willing to risk it all to find salvation. It was the righteousness that comes by faith that the Father saw, faithfully delivering her as the walls of Jericho came crashing down around them. It was a humble heart that the Father would nurture back to life in the care of the Israelite camp for years to come, building through Rahab direct descendents of men, from Boaz to King David, who would foreshadow the coming Christ and eventually bring Him into the world. Because what the Father saw in Rahab was not unforgivable sin, but the pain of her past, her great capacity to love and her faith to believe that He was a God to make life worth living.

13

Angels and Demons

The first time I attempted to write down our story, the Lord showed me like pieces of a puzzle how to lay out each and every chapter. Even the titles were inspired and I knew at that time there was a Chapter 13: *Angels and Demons*. But over the course of writing, I struggled with this chapter and for a time, decided not to include it. In my heart I believed that many would have trouble accepting this chapter, so in fear, I opted to leave it out.

However the Lord spoke to my heart again and made it plain that I was to tell the whole story, come what may, because it was the truth and a very real part of our lives today. It is the subject of spiritual warfare and what has happened for our family in more recent years.

Neal has always been aware of evil, as it's very

real presence pursued his family for years. He saw over and over again, Satan seemed to get the upper hand, cutting the lives short of close family members and bringing his entire family into ruin. I had just begun to learn of the real battle we were in when the Lord first called me to pray and intercede for Neal throughout his incarceration. After reading many books on spiritual warfare and from my own experiences with the demonic, I learned that the enemy was indeed prowling around, yet was made completely powerless with the name of Jesus. That name could send these beasts fleeing in a second and the child of God truly had that weapon at their disposal.

But that didn't keep Satan from trying to gain a foothold, whether it was through sin and rebellion against God or generational curses passed down from the sins of our fathers. I learned that sometimes what we need to overcome certain destructive tendencies in our life came down to an issue of deliverance, the enemy able to hold us hostage, even the Christian, simply because we have not learned how to fight on this front.

When the Lord first called me to intercessory prayer, I felt deep conviction to let go of the areas of my life that could lead me to stumble. Through the power of the Holy Spirit, I gave up some of the more obvious rebellious behaviors I had in my heart. The Lord burdened me with the need to strengthen my defenses so that the enemy would not be able to use my weaknesses against me as I prayed in warfare for Neal. Not that I became perfect, far from it, but the areas of my heart where I was aware of unrepentant sin, I shut and sealed the door.

The Lord led me to pray fervently and every night against unseen forces at work in Neal's life and as a result, Neal was radically delivered from the demons that had taught him to lie, steal and hurt people without remorse. The dark forces that led him back to drug abuse time and time again were finally defeated. Because Neal's family had such a long history of sin and abuse, Neal became knowledgeable in generational curses and was able to break them in the name of Jesus one by one. He survived because we learned how to fight in a different arena, not just what we and others could see but what was pulling the strings behind the scenes.

However, it wasn't until a year ago, that the Lord pulled back the veil even farther on a world I before could barely comprehend. I was going through a difficult time in my life, forced to make a painful decision and begging the Lord for guidance. Something I wanted desperately was also something I had to let go of out of obedience to Him.

In the midst of many tears, I cried out to the Lord that if life was to be about serving Him and letting go of things we want, then Lord, please, I asked Him, make it worth something. I prayed, Lord, give me all You got. If I was to make these types of sacrifices, I wanted to be more than just a good Christian. I wanted to see people radically saved and blessed. I prayed and asked God from the Scripture in Mark 16:17, 18, "And these signs will accompany those who believe: In my name they will drive out demons; they will speak in new tongues; they will pick up snakes with their hands; and when they drink deadly poison, it will not hurt them at all; they will place their hands on sick people, and they will get well." Minutes later I fell to my knees in prayer with surges of what felt like electricity going through my body. Face down on the floor for several minutes, I felt surge after surge pulse through me, moving my body as it passed through and when it was finally over, I sat up with tears streaming down my face. The presence of God was so thick and powerful; I was filled with incredible peace.

After that day, it was as if the dial had been turned up in my head. I could hear the Lord more clearly and He was teaching me new things about the kingdom of God that I had not fully understood before, like how incredibly close it is to us all the time. He showed me how hard He fights for us every second of the day and the immeasurable love He has for all of us. I had often felt like the Lord must look at me and shake His head in disappointment, but He assured me that was not the case at all. He knew our struggles and that we were all born into this fallen world and were lost without Him.

Jesus had not sat passively by, only grieving with us as we suffered but He was a great warrior King on the frontlines, fighting a battle all around us that we often couldn't see. Although the war was already won on the cross at Calvary, the enemy was not quick to give up ground and there were still strongholds that needed to be torn down one by one until He returns. He showed me there are many still held captive by a defeated enemy.

It was during this time of revelation, in late summer of 2012 that I began to pray for a friend of mine I will call Sara, who was suffering with ovarian cancer. Throughout her chemotherapy, I would visit on Saturdays to help in any way I could. Sara was a very spiritual person and steeped in New Age philosophies. Although she professed to believe in Jesus, she had also opened herself up to many false gods as well, Satan masquerading as a being of light.

During our time together, I laid hands on her and prayed for healing and in the course of our conversations; the Lord put a clear word for her in my heart: NO OTHER NAME. I saw these block letters in my head one day as I drove away from her house and so as soon as I arrived home, I contacted her and told her what the Lord had said. She responded in tears, and said that this word from God was not a surprise to her. Apparently the Lord was already revealing this truth, based on the Scripture in Acts 4:12, "Salvation is found in no one else, for there is no other name under heaven given to men by which we must be saved." So, in that moment, she claimed Jesus as Lord and began to pray for deliverance in the name of Jesus.

That same evening, Sara called me in distress. She let me know her house was in an uproar. Her cats were fighting and tearing at each other, items in her home were knocked over and broken and she was feeling new waves of illness. She quickly recognized that she was under demonic attack and continued to pray for deliverance in Jesus' name.

I didn't hear from her again for several months. I called every week to see if I could help in any way but she politely declined. I continued to pray for her, hoping that deliverance from the demonic activity around her would finally come.

The following November, I went to lay down in the back bedroom of my home for a nap and found I was again experiencing surges all over my body. I rolled off the bed and on to my knees to receive from God and there I saw a vision, two angels standing over me, each with an arm outstretched touching my back. I asked in prayer to see these angels with my eyes but was told that it would frighten me, so I stayed there in my posture of prayer until the surging stopped.

After that episode, the dial was again turned way up, and for a period of a couple of weeks, I was having intense visions, dreams and words from the Lord. He instructed me to fast, not telling me for how long, but only when to begin and the following day, I finally heard again from Sara. She asked me to come see her but not for any assistance, only to pray. This friend who had barely talked to me for months now wanted me to come pray for her, while I was fasting and in the midst of the most intense spiritual experiences of my life. I quickly said yes and waited to see what God would do.

That Saturday, as I entered her house still fasting, I felt led of the Lord to tell her everything that I had been experiencing for the last few days. I poured out my heart to her and then listened to her grieve over the many broken relationships and difficulties she was having in the final days of her life. The enemy had been raking her over the coals, and many of the "friends" she believed she had, were turning their back on her.

Jesus began to speak to her through me, telling her how much He loved her, how much He wanted to be there to prepare her meals and give her baths. Tears were streaming down my face to hear the declaration of love for her from the King. I laid hands on her and instantly my arms were moving

91

effortless without my direction. Her eyes widened as she felt these surges of the kingdom enter her body. We sat together and prayed, reveling in the presence of God. The very next day, God ended my fast.

Two days later, as I was laying my youngest in his bed, the Lord told me a new day was coming for Sara, even right at her door. I started to tremble and war in the Spirit, a cry from my spirit uttering the glory and power of God, as if a thousand angels had just drawn their swords and were running at all the demonic forces assigned to her. In an instant, the Lord said to me, *Sara has been healed.*

That night as I lay in my bed, I was awakened several times by commotion outside and the sound of wind as if a train were passing. When I went to the Lord in prayer, He told me that he was commanding angels to our property to protect our family. We would be under attack from the enemy as a result of the deliverance that had occurred that day for my friend. I asked the Lord if it would be safe to leave the property and He assured me these angels would be following our family everywhere we went.

The next morning, fearing to my core that I was losing my mind, I looked out the windows of our home, desperate to see evidence of angels and what the Lord had clearly told me the night before. I looked to Sara's physical condition for evidence that she had been delivered of demons. The Lord assured me that deliverance of demons *was* a healing. Sara had told me several times that she wanted to go to be with the Lord. She had suffered much abuse and was tired of this world. But still I struggled looking for a more tangible sign of deliverance.

As days passed and Sara's health continued to deteriorate, I huddled in a corner in my home and experienced one of the worst demonic attacks of my life. My mind was under assault, the enemy trying to convince me that I was crazy to believe there even was a Jesus. In the midst of massive panic attacks and wave after wave of demonic oppression, I heard the Lord whisper to me, *Hold on to what you know, Carrie. What do you know?* I began to make bold statements of faith. "I believe that Jesus is the Son of God. I believe He came to the earth two thousand years ago. I believe He walked this earth to become a sinless sacrifice for my sin. I believe He died and rose again and sits at the right hand of the Father..." and so on and with every statement of faith, the assault began to lift.

However, for days afterward I was, to put it mildly, a basket case. In my mind, I was either completely demonized, losing my mind or having an encounter with the kingdom of God that I had absolutely no frame of reference for. I cried for days at the possibility that I was crazy and so I was in this state on Thanksgiving Day, barely making it through the meal without falling apart in tears.

As my husband and I left the dinner, I cried uncontrollably in the passenger side of our car as he listened quietly to all my fears. Suddenly, he turned the car around and asked if I would be willing to go on a drive with him. I shook my head yes and waited as he drove us to a church property that had, high on a hill, a giant cross. He pointed to the cross and said to me, "Jesus just told me that what you are looking for is up there at the cross. I don't know what it is, I just know Jesus is going to meet you up there."

Still crying, I opened my car door and began my ascent to this cross. Passing through backyards and up a steep embankment, I finally reached the foot of the enormous symbol. I sat down, my back to it and asked the Lord audibly and with all sincerity, "What could You possibly show me up here that could convince me I am not losing my mind?!" He spoke quietly to me and said, *Turn around.* Slowly I turned to look up at the cross behind me and stared up at the sky.

Moments later I began to see them, balls of light streaming across the sky, shooting upwards, sideways, rising and falling against grey clouds. I blinked hard and looked again as the Lord whispered softly to me, *Angels, Carrie, and they follow you everywhere you go.* My mouth dropped open as I watched these orbs dance across the sky with purpose. The King was showing me our angels, proof to me that a great deliverance for Sara had taken place. With joy flooding my heart I descended back down the hill, looking over my shoulder to see the orbs fly and follow me down to the car.

Sara went on to be with the Lord but the angels have never left. I see them every day, flying circles around our car as we drive, rising and falling outside of the windows. I walk our property and see them clearly against the sky. To me, it is a reminder of the very real battle that we are in and of the incredible power and presence of God. I've grown accustomed to them now, but know what a gift the Lord has given one so undeserving. Still I am not sure why. It is not because I have done things well or in any way have earned it. It is not any kind of promotion based on merit. Every day, the attitudes of my heart remind me how desperately wicked I am.

Yet in recent months, I've been able to lay hands on others and see them get well. Not every time but more than ever before. Laying hands on my mother's lower back pain, my hands began to move involuntarily, pushing and commanding the enemy out for a full and complete healing. I've laid hands on my children and watched them get healed. I've even been able to pray over my own pain for instant healing. Not always, but more often than not and when led of the Holy Spirit, my prayers for healing get answered.

I don't pretend to know all the purposes God has for this. I know one thing for certain; it is only for the grace of God that I am able to stand here today, blessed, with a life I never dreamed possible. I love Him with every ounce of my being but I am only someone that has been willing to do what the King has asked. I am someone who knows how incapable I am of making good decisions on my own, so I stay in constant conversation with Him. I know whatever He asks me to do, no matter how difficult, will be worth it in the end because I know how much the Savior loves me. I know this because I am one of the least of these.

14

The Least of These

I am not special. I am not unique. Born of fire and adversity, I came to know the Lord on my knees, when the pain of life had become too excruciating for me to bear. I have not earned special favor, nor have I done anything to deserve the many blessings the Lord has heaped on me. What I am is a woman in love. Since the first moment Jesus came like a white knight to rescue me from an abusive marriage, I have adored Him.

There are many, many others who understand the Bible much better than I do, who have read it far more times than I have. There are many others who have accomplished far greater things than me. But this I know, when I finally did come back to the Lord, my head hung down and my heart disparaging, the Father ran to me, embraced me and has welcomed me home every day since. He is all that I trust in this world and I would do anything for

Him, even wait for a husband that was five years in the making.

Neal is the same way. He loves Jesus with all the ruggedness and courage of an embattled soldier. It was only Jesus that reached down into his hell to pull him out. It has been Jesus that has spoken to his heart every day since, healing the wounds and helping him back on his feet. Loyal to the end, Neal would die for Him in a heartbeat and is quick to obey anything the Lord whispers to his heart.

Neal can sometimes offend, the years of having to fight to survive still raising its head from time to time. He may not trust you right away; it may take time to get past his walls. He has a few tattoos, swears on occasion and struggles with forgiveness. But Neal would be the first to help if ever you were down and out, the first to give money to a homeless person on the street, often sensing them before I even know they are there. He follows God with all his heart and God often uses him, behind a bar or with his peers, to give hope to people that would not even consider darkening the door of a church. Neal is a soldier for the King, rough around the edges, but completely pure in heart.

And so the Lord says:

> *God blesses those who are poor and realize*
> *their need for him,*
> *for the Kingdom of Heaven is theirs.*
> *God blesses those who mourn,*
> *for they will be comforted.*
> *God blesses those who are humble,*
> *for they will inherit the whole earth.*
> *God blesses those who hunger and thirst for*
> *justice,*
> *for they will be satisfied.*

97

God blesses those who are merciful,
for they will be shown mercy.
God blesses those whose hearts are pure,
for they will see God.
                                    Matthew 5:3-8, NLT

It is the brokenhearted who have an advantage. In the despair of life, these poor in spirit have grabbed on to the Savior with both hands, determined not to let Him go, because they know without Him, they are lost. The Lord says for that, they receive the kingdom of heaven. All the bitter nights spent weeping, begging God for second chances, repenting from such depths that truly nothing of them is left; He says for those who mourn, they will be comforted.

Their hearts are tendered to the sadness of life, the torment that came when they followed their own path without regard for Him. They cannot exalt their own efforts but instead long for even the crumbs from the Master's table. For these meek, He gives the whole earth. They have been broken by inequities, felt the sting of self righteousness and been slaves to the sins of others; for that, they receive justice in full.

They are merciful, because they know what it is like to be lost. They know that they did not deserve the incredible kindness shown by the Lord and so they are quick to show that kindness to others; their hearts broken by what could have been. Their hearts are pure, even though outwardly at times they seem far from perfect, because they know that in the end, His love is all that truly matters.

It is why so often Jesus held company with the outcasts of society. He was able to speak to them in ways He could not speak to others, their hearts broken and thirsty for some Good News. It is why Jesus said to the religious leaders, "I tell you the truth, the tax collectors and the prostitutes are entering the kingdom of God ahead of you. For John (the Baptist) came to you to show you the way of righteousness, and you did not believe him, but the tax collectors and the prostitutes did." (*Matt 21: 31, 32*). They are desperate for salvation and hungry for freedom. It is why Jesus tells Simon, the Pharisee, this story:

> *"Two men owed money to a certain moneylender. One owed him five hundred denarii and the other fifty. Neither of them had the money to pay him back, so he canceled the debts of both. Now which of them will love him more?"*
>
> *Simon replied, "I suppose the one who had the bigger debt canceled."*
>
> *"You have judged correctly," Jesus said. Then he turned toward the woman and said to Simon, "Do you see this woman? I came into your house. You did not give me any water for my feet, but she wet my feet with her tears and wiped them with her hair. You did not give me a kiss, but this woman, from the time I entered, has not stopped kissing my feet. You did not put oil on my head, but she has poured perfume on my feet. Therefore, I tell you, her many sins have been forgiven—for she loved much. But he who has been forgiven little loves little."*
>
> *Luke 7: 41-47*

They know what it is to love Him, deeply and without measure for all He has done for them; their lives poured out as an offering on His feet. They bleed and they yearn for Him as the source of life and don't question Him when He asks anything of them. He is the King and He need not prove His immeasurable goodness to them. And when the King asks them to lose their life in order to find true life, it is much easier for them to do. The brokenhearted ones have an advantage, a lesson to be taught with their lives and a lesson the church desperately needs.

The woman coming out of a life of prostitution, radically saved attempts the local church. Her skirts are too short because that is the only way she knows how to dress. She swears as she fumbles for her keys and smokes in the parking lot. Eyes glance her direction but pretend not to see her, hoping she will not sit too closely to them.

A convicted felon sits in the back row at church, his clothes worn and smelling like booze, he has promised to change his life if given a second chance. He feels the weight of the stares of well groomed families smiling uncomfortably and giving him a wide berth. He leaves halfway through the service, feeling stupid for even attempting a church, clearly more sinful from those around him.

A single mom cries through worship, feeling the love of a Father in a way she never has before. She hears that to be a part of the church she will have to join a small group, but the thought of sitting in a room with "normal" couples and sharing her life story causes her to run again to the safety of the bar, a place where she knows she will be accepted.

These precious ones are lost over and over again. Yet with a few words spoken in love, a gentle touch, and a welcoming face, these ones can be moved in an instant to stay. If that same face would call them, take them out to dinner, and invite them to church the following Sunday, then maybe they might believe the church was a place for them.

The Bible says Jesus had dinner with the outcasts of society. He spent time with the thieves, the prostitutes, the adulterous, the addicted, the homeless, and the demonized. It was something so simple but so revolutionary that the religious leaders were astounded. He cast demons out of shattered lives and restored them with a word. He did not merely volunteer for ministries to the poor and afflicted, but He made it personal at great risk to Himself.

He knew it wasn't a ministry or a program or a support group alone that brought life to the lost. It was the encouragement and unconditional love of someone who could speak Jesus into their life. It was the power of the kingdom of God that could loose the captive. It was people that were willing to take great risk, to align themselves with brokenness so that a life might be saved, in spite of all the ugliness, difficulties and demonic attack it would bring.

The broken flocked to Jesus because He had love written all over His face. He saw past all their flaws to the perfect creation He designed. He picked them out from the dirt of the world, wiped them off through tears, and held their hand until they were safely home. These gems require our arms around them in love as well; with hands held high asking God to show us how to fight the enemy on their behalf. We must treat them with the special favor they so deserve for all they have overcome. Are we willing to learn from them, esteeming them as better than ourselves and allowing ourselves to be changed by a God in the trenches?

The Master sees a mighty Christian warrior, a survivor who has met the King and someone for whom the red carpet should be rolled out. As with the prodigal son, the Lord offers the "fatted calf" for the ones who have gone astray, having survived their circumstances to find their way to their knees in powerful repentance (*Luke 15:11-32*). Their lives have so much to offer and to teach. They should not be seen as perpetually broken, but powerful instruments of righteousness Christ will use to accomplish His purposes on the earth, like He has done for so many before- Mary Magdalene, the demoniac of the tombs, the adulterous woman, Matthew the tax collector, the Samaritan woman of the well, Rahab the prostitute. We should be honored by their presence.

Paul writes in 1 Corinthians 12: 18- 26:

> *But in fact God has arranged the parts in the body, every one of them, just as he wanted them to be. If they were all one part, where would the body be? As it is, there are many parts, but one body.*
> *The eye cannot say to the hand, "I don't need you!" And the head cannot say to the feet, "I don't need you!" On the contrary, those parts of the body that seem to be weaker are* <u>indispensable</u>, *and the parts that we think are less honorable we treat with* <u>special honor</u>. *And the parts that are*

unpresentable are treated with <u>special modesty</u>, while our presentable parts need no special treatment. But God has combined the members of the body and has· given <u>greater honor to the parts that lacked it</u>, so that there should be no division in the body, but that its parts should have equal concern for each other. If one part suffers, every part suffers with it; if one part is honored, every part rejoices with it.

The "least of these" are indispensable to the church because they are the heartbeat of God; His special trophies won back from the enemy. He feasts and celebrates over them. Like the lost sheep, He has sought them out and is overjoyed to have them back in the fold.

Yet over and over again, they get lost in the church amid uncomfortable glances, lovelessness, and lack of prayer. The voice of the Pharisee echoes through the church corridors, "God, I thank you that I am not like other men- robbers, evildoers, adulterers- or even like this tax collector. I fast twice a week and give a tenth of all I get." (*Luke 18:11*). But what does the Lord say about these seemingly devastated lives? "But the tax collector (or divorcee, convicted felon, alcoholic) stood at a distance. He would not even look up to heaven, but beat his breast and said, 'God, have mercy on me, a sinner" (*Luke 18:13*). Who goes home justified before God? The one who knows he is a sinner.

Perhaps it is the ones seen as most broken and damaged that can teach us the most about what it means to be humble before God. Perhaps it is these broken hearted ones that have been brought low, that teach us how to truly kneel.

Although at times, they can be difficult. They may not speak Christian. Words like fellowship and community do not come easy to them. They will not immediately let down the defenses that helped them survive in the world for years. They will not show up at small groups and tell their sordid stories, and if they do, it is a momentous triumph. Many would rather stay home than face the potential disdain. The enemy is always quick to use their past against them and shame often keeps them hidden. Sometimes they are difficult to find, standing in the shadows of the church, often times going unnoticed.

Sometimes they have not yet broken free of sinful patterns, or even know that they are in them. They don't need to constantly be reminded of their sin. What they long for is unconditional love and acceptance, a believer pointing them to Jesus and letting the Holy Spirit bring conviction, repentance and the power to overcome. They take extra effort and need a lot of encouragement, gentle coaxing to prove goodness and sincerity, and faithful persistent prayer. At times they will need patience and sometimes, forgiveness, when they say and do all the wrong things. They know the difference between a nice gesture and an act of love. They can quickly perceive self righteousness in others and know when they are not seen as equal. They can smell a false front a mile away, but the smallest act of genuine love can go a long way.

They need the standard bearers of the church, those that are the fruit of generations of families that have served the Lord faithfully. They teach the broken hearted what life can really be like, what the fruit of the Spirit looks like on people and in families. At times, and through relationship, they will need loving correction from those faithful as the remnants of a former life attempt to rear its ugly head. They may need intercession and the laying on of hands, to deliver them from an enemy that is always looking for control. But most of all, they will need love and arms from the church that reflect the heart of Jesus, embracing them with special attention and kindness. For we are all one body, and when one hurts, we all hurt. And in loving the broken hearted, Jesus promises us this:

> *"Then the King will say to those on his right, 'Come, you who are blessed by my Father; take your inheritance, the kingdom prepared for you since the creation of the world. For I was hungry and you gave me something to eat, I was thirsty and you gave me something to drink, I was a stranger and you invited me in, I needed clothes and you clothed me, I was sick and you looked after me, I was in prison and you came to visit me.' Then the righteous will answer him, 'Lord, when did we see you hungry and feed you, or thirsty and give you something to drink? When did we see you a stranger and invite you in, or needing clothes and clothe you? When did we see you sick or in prison and go to visit you?' The King will reply, 'Truly I tell you, whatever you did for one of the least of these brothers and sisters of mine, you did for me.'"*

> *Matthew 25:34-40*

O King, teach us how to love our brother!

Epilogue

We all sin. We all fall short. But praise God that it is not up to us to accomplish all His purposes. It is only up to us to surrender. When He shows us we are desperate, that we need Him, it is only for us to fall on our knees and ask the King for help. When we suffer from deep and perpetual sin, from drug abuse to self-righteousness, it is only the name of Jesus that brings true and lasting freedom. So call out to Him we must and sometimes, over and over again.

When our lives are messy, may we cling to Him. When we fail over and over again, may we reach for Him. Let us not be discouraged but take heart that when we earnestly pursue and seek Him; when our hearts are turned to Him even when our lives are ugly, it will all end well. He is faithful to fulfill all His promises to us.

Let's pray together:

King Jesus,

I come now with all the weight and ugliness of my sin before You. I lay it at Your feet and ask You to forgive me. I believe now that You love me, that You died upon the cross for me and I ask You now to please come into my heart and be my Savior. Protect me from all the attacks of the enemy that will surely come as a result of my allegiance to You. Give me eyes to see when temptation comes my way. I renounce any ways I have allowed Satan to control and dominate my thoughts. Unearth the lies in my head and replace them with Your truth.

Father, when I fail You and want to run and hide, remind me that I can always turn to You and that You are always there beside me. Help me not to lose heart in dark places but comfort me in Your love. And if it takes days, months and years for me to receive all that You have for me on this earth, may I be faithful to You and not give up. All my hope is in You now and I surrender all.

In the mighty name of Jesus, I pray.

Amen.

For further information or prayer, feel free to contact us at
carrieandnealrozema@gmail.com

Blessings!

Made in the USA
Charleston, SC
27 February 2014